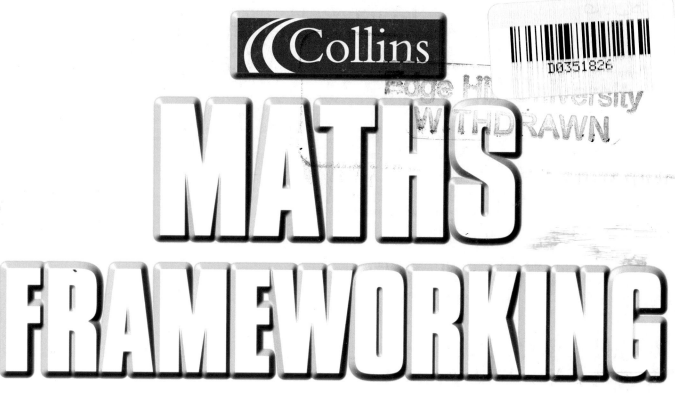

Collins

MATHS FRAMEWORKING

Complete success for Mathematics at KS3

| YEAR 8 | PUPIL BOOK 1 |

627343

KEVIN EVANS   KEITH GORDON   TREVOR SENIOR   BRIAN SPEED

Contents

CHAPTER 1

Number and Algebra 1

This chapter is going to show you

- how to multiply and divide negative numbers
- how to find the highest common factor and the lowest common multiple of sets of numbers
- how to find the prime factors of a number
- what square numbers and square roots are
- how to generate and describe number patterns

What you should already know

- How to add and subtract negative integers
- How to generate terms of a simple number sequence
- Recognise the square and triangle number sequences
- How to test numbers for divisibility

Multiplying and dividing negative numbers

Example 1.1   Work out the answers to   **a**   –2 – +4   **b**   –6 – –3 + –2

   a   Rewrite as –2 – 4 and count along a number line –2 – 4 = –6

–7   –6   –5   –4   –3   –2   –1   0   –1

   b   Rewrite as –6 + 3 – 2 and count along a number line –6 + 3 – 2 = –5

–7   –6   –5   –4   –3   –2   –1   0   –1

Example 1.2   Work out the answers to   **a** –2 × +4   **b** –6 × –3   **c** –15 ÷ –5   **d** +6 × –4 ÷ –2

   a   2 × 4 = 8, and – × + is equivalent to –. So, –2 × +4 = –8

   b   6 × 3 = 18, and – × – is equivalent to +. So, –6 × –3 = +18

   c   15 ÷ 5 = 3, and – ÷ – is equivalent to +. So, –15 ÷ –5 = +3

   d   +6 × –4 = –24, –24 ÷ –2 = +12

Example 1.3   Find the missing number in   **a** ☐ × 3 = –6   **b** –12 ÷ ☐ = 3

   a   The inverse problem is ☐ = –6 ÷ +3. So, the missing number is –2

   b   The inverse problem is ☐ = –12 ÷ +3. So, the missing number is –4.

1 Copy each of these calculations to show the pattern in each list of answers. Then fill in the missing numbers.

   a   3 + +1 = 4   **b**   −2 − +1 = −3   **c**   4 − +2 = 2
         3 + 0 = 3   −2 − 0 = −2   3 − +1 = 2
         3 + −1 = 2   −2 − −1 = −1   2 − 0 = 2
         3 + −2 = ...   −2 − −2 = ...   1 − −1 = ...
         3 + ... = ...   −2 − ... = ...   0 − ... = ...
         3 + ... = ...   −2 − ... = ... − ... = ...

2 Work out the answer to each of these.

   a   +3 − +2   **b**   −4 − −3   **c**   +7 − −6   **d**   −7 + −3
   e   +7 − +3   **f**   −9 − −5   **g**   −6 + +6   **h**   +6 − −7
   i   −6 + −6   **j**   −1 + −8   **k**   +5 − +7   **l**   7 − −5
   m   −2 − −3 + −4   **n**   − +1 + +1 − +2

3 Find the missing number to make each of these true.

   a   +2 + −6 = ☐   **b**   +4 + ☐ = +7   **c**   −4 + ☐ = 0
   d   +5 + ☐ = −1   **e**   +3 + +4 = ☐   **f**   ☐ − −5 = +7
   g   ☐ − +5 = +2   **h**   +6 + ☐ = 0   **i**   ☐ − −5 = −2
   j   +2 + −2 = ☐   **k**   ☐ − +2 = − 4   **l**   −2 + −4 = ☐

4 Work out each of these.

   a   −7 + 8   **b**   −2 − 7   **c**   +6 − 2 + 3   **d**   −6 − 1 + 7   **e**   −3 + 4 − 9
   f   −3 − 7   **g**   −4 + − 6   **h**   +7 − +6   **i**   −3 − 7 + −8   **j**   −5 + −4 − −7

5 In these 'walls', subtract the number in the right-hand brick from the number in the left-hand brick to find the number in the brick below.

   a 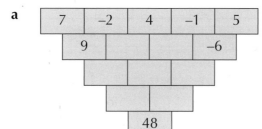   **b**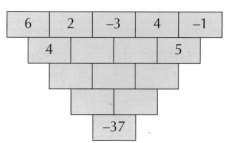

6 Copy and complete each of the following patterns.

   a   3 × +3 = 9   **b**   3 × −2 = −6   **c**   −2 × +1 = −2
         2 × +3 = 6   2 × −2 = −4   −1 × +1 = ...
         1 × +3 = ...   1 × −2 = ... × +1 = ...
         0 × +3 = ...   0 × −2 = ... × +1 = ...
         ...... × +3 = ... × −2 = ... × +1 = ...
         ...... × +3 = ... × −2 = ... × +1 = ...

7 Work out the answer to each of these.

a	$+2 \times -3$	**b**	$-3 \times +4$	**c**	$-5 \times +2$	**d**	-6×-3
e	$-3 \times +8$	**f**	$-4 \times +5$	**g**	-3×-4	**h**	-6×-1
i	$+7 \times -2$	**j**	$+2 \times +8$	**k**	$+6 \times -10$	**l**	$+8 \times +4$
m	-15×-2	**n**	$-6 \times -3 \times -1$	**o**	$-2 \times +4 \times -2$		

8 Work out the answer to each of these.

a	$+12 \div -3$	**b**	$-24 \div +4$	**c**	$-6 \div +2$	**d**	$-6 \div -3$
e	$-32 \div +8$	**f**	$-40 \div +5$	**g**	$-32 \div -4$	**h**	$-6 \div -1$
i	$+7 \div -2$	**j**	$+12 \div +6$	**k**	$+60 \div -10$	**l**	$+8 \div +4$
m	$-15 \div -2$	**n**	$-6 \times -3 \div -2$	**o**	$-2 \times +6 \div -3$		

9 Find the missing number in each calculation. (Remember: numbers without a + or – sign in front are always positive.)

a $2 \times -3 = \square$

b $-2 \times \square = -8$

c $3 \times \square = -9$

d $\square \div -5 = -15$

e $-4 \times -6 = \square$

f $-3 \times \square = -24$

g $-64 \div \square = 32$

h $\square \times 6 = 36$

i $-2 \times 3 = \square$

Extension Work

This is an algebraic magic square.

Find the value in each cell when $a = 7$, $b = 9$, $c = 2$.

Find the value in each cell when $a = -1$, $b = -3$, $c = -5$.

$a+c$	$c-a-b$	$b+c$
$b+c-a$	c	$a+c-b$
$c-b$	$a+b+c$	$c-a$

HCF and LCM

Remember:

    HCF stands for Highest Common Factor

    LCM stands for Lowest Common Multiple

Look at the diagrams below. What do you think they are showing?

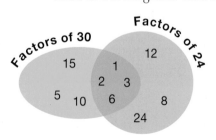

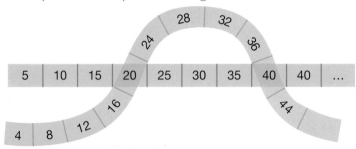

Example 1.4 ▷ Find the lowest common multiple (LCM) of the following pairs of numbers.

    a   3 and 7   **b**   6 and 9

    a   Write out the first few multiples of each number:

            3, 6, 9, 12, 15, 18, (21), 24, 27, …

            7, 14, (21), 28, 35, …

        You can see that the LCM of 3 and 7 is 21.

    b   Write out the multiples of each number:

            6, 12, (18), 24, …

            9, (18), 27, 36,

        You can see that the LCM of 6 and 9 is 18.

Example 1.5 ▷ Find the highest common factor (HCF) of the following pairs of numbers.

    a   15 and 21   **b**   16 and 24

    a   Write out the factors of each number: 1, (3), 5, 15

                                              1, (3), 7, 21

        You can see that the HCF of 15 and 21 is 3.

    b   Write out the factors of each number: 1, 2, 4, (8), 16

                                              1, 2, 3, 4, 6, (8), 12, 24

        You can see that the HCF of 16 and 24 is 8.

Exercise 1B

1 Write down the numbers in the row below that are multiples of:

    a   2   **b**   3   **c**   5   **d**   10

10	4	23	18	69	81	8	65	33	72	100

2 Write down the first ten multiples of:

    a   4   **b**   5   **c**   8   **d**   9   **e**   10

3 Write out all the factors of:

    a   15   **b**   20   **c**   32   **d**   12   **e**   25

4 Use your answers to Question 2 to help to find the LCM of:

    a   5 and 8   **b**   4 and 10   **c**   4 and 9   **d**   8 and 10

5 Use your answers to Question 3 to help to find the HCF of:

    a   15 and 20   **b**   15 and 25   **c**   12 and 20   **d**   20 and 32

6 Find the LCM of:

    a   5 and 9   **b**   5 and 25   **c**   3 and 8   **d**   4 and 6

    e   8 and 12   **f**   12 and 15   **g**   9 and 21   **h**   7 and 11

    [**Hint:** Write out the multiples of each number.]

7 Find the HCF of:

a	15 and 18	**b**	12 and 32	**c**	12 and 22	**d**	8 and 12
e	2 and 18	**f**	8 and 18	**g**	18 and 27	**h**	7 and 11

[**Hint:** Write out the factors of each number.]

Extension Work

The square numbers are 1, 4, 9, 16, 25, 36, ...

The triangle numbers are 1, 3, 6, 10, 15, 21, 28, 36, ...

The first number that is common to both series is 1.

What are the next two numbers that are common to both sequences?

You might find a spreadsheet useful to help you to solve this.

Square numbers and square roots

You have met square numbers in Pupil Book 1 for Year 7 (page 109). For example, $5^2 = 5 \times 5 = 25$.

The opposite of the square of a number is its square root. This is shown by the sign $\sqrt{}$. For example, $\sqrt{25} = 5$.

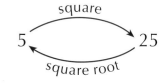

The following table gives the square roots of the square numbers up to 144.

You will have to learn these.

Square number	1	4	9	16	25	36	49	64	81	100	121	144
Square root	1	2	3	4	5	6	7	8	9	10	11	12

Example 1.6 Work out the answer to   **a** $\sqrt{4} \times \sqrt{36}$ **b** $\sqrt{144} \div \sqrt{4}$

a $\sqrt{4} \times \sqrt{36} = 2 \times 6 = 12$

b $\sqrt{144} \div \sqrt{4} = 12 \div 2 = 6$

Example 1.7 Use your calculator to find   **a** $\sqrt{729}$ **b** $\sqrt{1000}$

a Calculators work in different ways. On some calculators, you have to key the number first and then press the square root key $\sqrt{}$. On others, you have to press the square root key before pressing the number key.

The answer is 27. Make sure you know how to use your calculator.

b The answer is 31.622 776 6. You may round this to 32 or 31.6.

1 $3^2 + 4^2 = 5^2$ is an example of a *special square sum* (made up of only square numbers). There are many to be found. See which of the following pairs of squares will give you a special square sum.

$5^2 + 12^2$ $3^2 + 7^2$ $6^2 + 8^2$ $5^2 + 12^2$

$5^2 + 9^2$ $10^2 + 24^2$ $7^2 + 24^2$

2 Write down the value represented by each of the following. Do not use a calculator.

a $\sqrt{16}$	**b** $\sqrt{36}$	**c** $\sqrt{4}$	**d** $\sqrt{49}$	**e** $\sqrt{1}$
f $\sqrt{9}$	**g** $\sqrt{100}$	**h** $\sqrt{81}$	**i** $\sqrt{25}$	**j** $\sqrt{64}$

3 Work out each of these.

a $\sqrt{4} \times \sqrt{9}$ **b** $\sqrt{64} \div \sqrt{4}$ **c** $\sqrt{81} \div \sqrt{9}$ **d** $\sqrt{100} \times \sqrt{144}$

e $\sqrt{25} \times \sqrt{9}$ **f** $\sqrt{49} \times \sqrt{9}$ **g** $\sqrt{25} \times \sqrt{4} \times \sqrt{81}$ **h** $\sqrt{100} \times \sqrt{81} \div \sqrt{36}$

4 With the aid of a calculator, write down the value represented by each of the following.

a $\sqrt{289}$	**b** $\sqrt{961}$	**c** $\sqrt{529}$	**d** $\sqrt{2500}$	**e** $\sqrt{1296}$
f $\sqrt{729}$	**g** $\sqrt{3249}$	**h** $\sqrt{361}$	**i** $\sqrt{3969}$	**j** $\sqrt{1764}$

5 Make an estimate of each of the following square roots. Then use your calculator to see how many you got right.

a $\sqrt{256}$	**b** $\sqrt{1089}$	**c** $\sqrt{625}$	**d** $\sqrt{2704}$	**e** $\sqrt{1444}$
f $\sqrt{841}$	**g** $\sqrt{3481}$	**h** $\sqrt{441}$	**i** $\sqrt{4096}$	**j** $\sqrt{2025}$

6 Use a calculator to work out each of the following. Round each answer to the nearest whole number:

a $\sqrt{300}$	**b** $\sqrt{500}$	**c** $\sqrt{200}$	**d** $\sqrt{450}$	**e** $\sqrt{10}$

Extension Work

1 **a** Choose any two square numbers: for example, m and n.

b Multiply them together: $m \times n = R$.

c What is the square root of this result, $\sqrt{R}$?

d Can you find a connection between this square root and the two starting numbers?

e Try this again for more square numbers.

f Is the connection the same no matter what two square numbers you choose?

2 See if you can find any more sets of the special square sums.

Prime factors

What are the prime factors of 120 and 210?

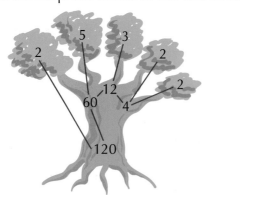 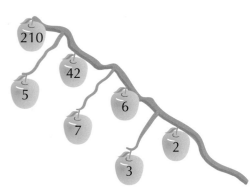

Example 1.8 Find the prime factors of 18.

Using a prime factor tree, split 18 into 3×6 and 6 into 3×2.

So, $18 = 2 \times 3 \times 3$.

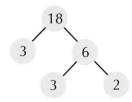

Exercise 1D

1 These are the prime factors of some numbers. What are the numbers?

    a $2 \times 2 \times 3$ **b** $2 \times 3 \times 3 \times 5$ **c** $2 \times 2 \times 3 \times 3$ **d** $2 \times 3 \times 5$ **e** $2 \times 2 \times 5$

2 Using a prime factor tree, work out the prime factors of:

    a 8   **b** 10   **c** 16   **d** 20   **e** 28
    f 34   **g** 35   **h** 40   **i** 50   **j** 100

3 Use a prime factor tree to work out the prime factors of each of the following.
(To help you, a starting multiplication is given.)

    a 42 (6×7) **b** 75 (5×15) **c** 140 (7×20) **d** 250 (5×50)
    e 480 (60×8) **f** 72 (8×9) **g** 96 (4×24) **h** 256 (4×64)

Extension Work

Make a poster showing the prime factors of a large number, such as 400. Draw a picture of a real tree like that at the start of this section.

Sequences 1

Example 1.9

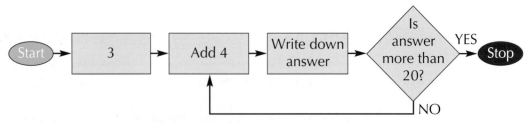

Follow through the above flow diagram and write down the numbers generated.
These are 3, 7, 11, 15, 19, 23.

Example 1.10 ▷ For each of the following sequences: **i** find the term-to-term rule, and **ii** find the next two terms.

a 2, 6, 10, 14, 18, 22, …   **b** 1, 3, 27, 81, 243, …

i 4 is added to next term.   **i** Each term is multiplied by 3 to get
So the term-to term-rule is +4   the next term. So, the term-to-term
                                                rule is × 3.

ii The next two terms are 26, 30.   **ii** The next two terms are 729, 2187.

Exercise 1E

1 Follow each set of instructions to generate a sequence:

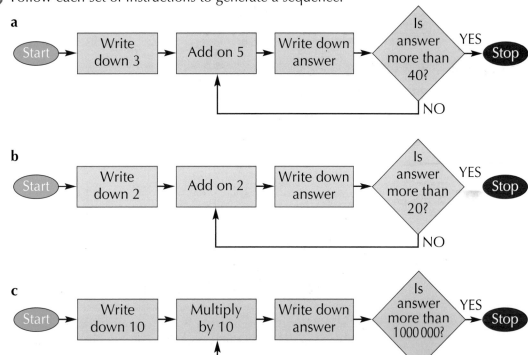

a

b

c

2 a What is the name of the sequence of numbers generated by the flow diagram in Question 1, part **b**?

b Draw a flow diagram to generate the odd numbers 1, 3, 5, 7, 9, 11.

3 a Describe the sequence of numbers generated by the flow diagram in Question 1, part **c**.

b Draw a flow diagram to generate the sequence of powers of 2 (2, 4, 8, 16, 32, 64, …).

4 Find the term-to-term rule for each of the sequences below.

    a 1, 4, 7, 10, 13, 16, …   **b** 1, 4, 16, 64, 256, 1024, …
    c 1, 4, 8, 13, 19, 26, …   **d** 1, 4, 9, 16, 25, 36, …

5 Write down four sequences beginning 1, 5, …. Explain how each of them is generated.

6 Find the term-to-term rule for each of the following sequences. Write down the next two terms.

   a   40, 41, 43, 46, 50, 55, …   **b**   90, 89, 87, 84, 80, 75, …

   c   1, 3, 7, 13, 21, 31, …   **d**   2, 6, 12, 20, 30, 42, …

7 The following four patterns of dots generate sequences of numbers.

   i   Draw the next two patterns of dots in each case.

   ii Write down the next four numbers in each sequence.

a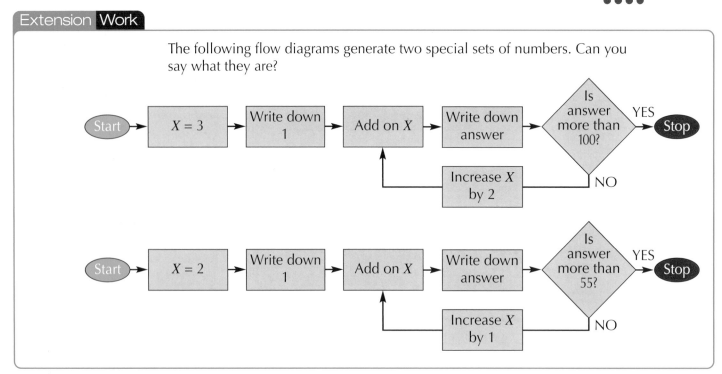

Extension **Work**

The following flow diagrams generate two special sets of numbers. Can you say what they are?

Start → $X = 3$ → Write down 1 → Add on X → Write down answer → Is answer more than 100? — YES → Stop
                                        ↑   │ NO
                                   Increase X by 2 ←──────────────────────┘

Start → $X = 2$ → Write down 1 → Add on X → Write down answer → Is answer more than 55? — YES → Stop
                                        ↑   │ NO
                                   Increase X by 1 ←──────────────────────┘

Sequences 2

Paving slabs, 1 metre square, are used to put borders around square ponds. For example:

1 × 1 m² pond
8 slabs

2 × 2 m² pond
12 slabs

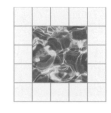

3 × 3 m² pond
16 slabs

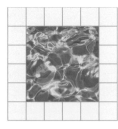

4 × 4 m² pond
20 slabs

How many slabs would fit around a 5 × 5 m² pond? What about a 100 × 100 m² pond?

Example 1.11 ▷ Write down **i** the first term and **ii** the constant difference of each of these sequences.

a 3, 7, 11, 15, 19, 23, ...   **b** 5, 8, 11, 14, 17, 20, 23, ...

a First term is 3. The constant difference is 4.

b First term is 5. The constant difference is 3.

Example 1.12 ▷ Using the term-to-term rules given, generate each of these sequences.

a First term 5, term-to-term rule is + 6.

b First term 32, term-to-term rule is × $\frac{1}{2}$.

c First term 3, term-to-term rule is subtract 1 then multiply by 2.

a The sequence is 5, 5 + 6 = 11, 11 + 6 = 17, ... This gives 5, 11, 17, 23, 29, 35, ...

b The sequence is 32 × $\frac{1}{2}$ = 16, 16 × $\frac{1}{2}$ = 8. This gives 32, 16, 8, 4, 2, 1, $\frac{1}{2}$, $\frac{1}{4}$, ...

c The sequence is (3 – 1) × 2 = 4, (4 – 1) × 2 = 6, (6 – 1) × 2 = 10 .... This gives 3, 4, 6, 10, 18, 34, 66, ...

Example 1.13 ▷ Write down the first five terms of each of the following sequences.

a 3 × term position number + 4   **b** 5n – 1, where n is the term position number

a First term is 3 × 1 + 4 = 7, second term is 3 × 2 + 4 = 10, third term = 3 × 3 + 4 = 13, fourth term is 3 × 4 + 4 = 16, fifth term is 3 × 5 + 4 = 19.

So, the sequence is 7, 10, 13, 16, 19, ...

b n = 1 gives 5 × 1 – 1 = 4, n = 2 gives 5 × 2 – 1 = 9, n = 3 gives 5 × 3 – 1 = 14, n = 4 gives 5 × 4 – 1 = 19, n = 5 gives 5 × 5 – 1 = 24.

So, the sequence is 4, 9, 14, 19, 24, ...

Exercise 1F

1 For each of the following sequences, write down the first term, and the constant difference:

a 4, 9, 14, 19, 24, 29, ...   **b** 1, 3, 5, 7, 9, 11, ...

c 3, 9, 15, 21, 27, 33, ...   **d** 5, 3, 1, –1, –3, –5, ...

2 Given the first term a and the constant difference d, write down the first six terms of each of these sequences:

a a = 1, d = 7   **b** a = 3, d = 2   **c** a = 5, d = 4

d a = 0.5, d = 1.5   **e** a = 4, d = –3   **f** a = 2, d = –0.5

3 Write down the first five terms of each of these sequences.

a First term 3   Term-to-term rule: Multiply by 2

b First term 4   Term-to-term rule: Multiply by 3 and add 1

c First term 5   Term-to-term rule: Subtract 1 and multiply by 2

4 The position-to-term definition of each of four sequences is given below. Use this to write down the first five terms of each sequence.

    a $2 \times$ (term position number) $- 1$ **b** $3 \times$ (term position number) $+ 1$

    c $4 \times$ (term position number) $+ 2$ **d** $2 \times$ (term position number) $+ 3$

5 The nth term of a sequence is given by a rule below. Use each rule to write down the first five terms of its sequence.

    a $4n + 1$ **b** $3n + 2$ **c** $3n - 2$ **d** $2n + 1$

Extension Work

Fibonacci numbers

You will need a calculator.

The Fibonacci sequence is: 1, 1, 2, 3, 5, 8, 13, 21, …

It is formed by adding together the previous two terms, that is $5 = 3 + 2$, $8 = 5 + 3$, etc.

Write down the next five terms of the sequence.

Now divide each term by the previous term, that is $1 \div 1 = 1$, $2 \div 1 = 2$, $3 \div 2 = 1.5$, $5 \div 3 = \ldots$

You should notice something happening.

You may find a computer spreadsheet useful for this activity.

If you have access to the Internet, find out about the Italian mathematician after whom the sequence is named.

Solving problems

An Investigation

At the start of the last section, you were asked to find the number of slabs that would be needed to go round a square pond of a certain size.

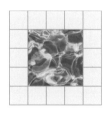

1 × 1 m² pond
8 slabs

2 × 2 m² pond
12 slabs

3 × 3 m² pond
16 slabs

4 × 4 m² pond
20 slabs

To solve this problem you need to:

Step 1 Break down the problem into simple stages.

Step 2 Set up a table of results.

Step 3 Predict and test a rule.

Step 4 Use your rule to answer the question.

Step 1 This has been done already with the diagrams given.

Step 2

Pond size (m²)	Number of slabs
1 × 1	8
2 × 2	12
3 × 3	16
4 × 4	20

Step 3 Use the table to spot how the sequence is growing. In this case, it is increasing in 4s.

So, a 5 × 5m² pond will need 24 slabs as shown on the right.

You can also see that the number of slabs (S) is 4 times the side length of the pond (P) plus 4. This can be given as:

$$S = 4P + 4$$

Step 4 Now use the rule for the 100 × 100m² pond, where P = 100:

$$S = 4 \times 100 + 4 = 404$$

So, 404 slabs will be needed.

Exercise 1G

Do the following investigations. Make sure you follow the steps given above and explain clearly what you are doing. In each investigation you are given some hints.

1 Write a rule to show how many square slabs it takes to make a border around rectangular ponds.

 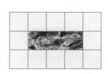 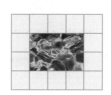

First side	Second side	Slabs
1	2	10
1	3	12
2	3	14

2 The final score in a football match was 5–4. How many different half-time scores could there have been?

For a match that ended 0–0, there is only one possible half-time result (0–0).

For a match that ended 1–2, there are six possible half-time scores (0–0, 0–1, 0–2, 1–0, 1–1, 1–2)

Take some other low-scoring matches, such as 1–1, 2–1, 2–0, etc., and work out the half-time scores for these.

Set up a table like the one in Question 1.

What you need to know for level 5

- How to multiply and divide decimals by 10, 100 and 1000
- How to add, subtract, multiply and divide using negative and positive numbers

National Curriculum SATs questions

LEVEL 4

1 *1998 Paper 2*

Owen has some tiles like these:

He uses the tiles to make a series of patterns.

Pattern number
1

Pattern number
2

Pattern number
3

Pattern number
4

a Each new pattern has more tiles than the one before. The number of tiles goes up by the same amount each time.

How many more tiles does Owen add each time he makes a new pattern?

b How many tiles will Owen need altogether to make pattern number 6?

c How many tiles will Owen need altogether to make pattern number 9?

d Owen uses 40 tiles to make a pattern. What is the number of the pattern he makes?

2 *2000 Paper 2*

   a Write down the next two numbers in the sequence below.

       281, 287, 293, 299, …, …

   b Write down the next two numbers in the sequence below.

       1, 4, 9, 16, 25, …, …

   c Describe the pattern in part **b** in your own words.

LEVEL 5

3 *1996 Paper 2*

This is a series of patterns with grey and black tiles.

  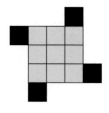

   a How many grey tiles and black tiles will there be in pattern number 8?

Pattern number 1

Pattern number 2

Pattern number 3

   b How many grey tiles and black tiles will there be in pattern number 16?

4 *2002 Paper 1*

Copy and complete these calculations by filling in the missing numbers in the boxes using only negative numbers.

$$\boxed{} - \boxed{} = 5 \qquad \boxed{} - \boxed{} = -5$$

5 *1999 Paper 2*

Jeff makes a sequence of patterns with black and grey triangular tiles.

Pattern number 1   Pattern number 2   Pattern number 3

The rule for finding the number of tiles in pattern number N in Jeff's sequence is:

      number of tiles = $1 + 3N$

   a The 1 in this rule represents the black tile.

      What does the $3N$ represent?

   b Jeff makes pattern number 12 in his sequence.

      How many black tiles and how many grey tiles does he use?

This chapter is going to show you

- how to identify parallel and perpendicular lines
- how to measure and draw reflex angles
- how to calculate angles in triangles
- how to use the properties of quadrilaterals
- how to draw triangles accurately

What you should already know

- How to draw and measure lines to the nearest millimetre
- How to draw and measure acute and obtuse angles
- The names of the different types of quadrilateral
- How to recognise shapes that have reflective and rotational symmetry

Parallel and perpendicular lines

Example 2.1 ▷ These two lines are parallel.

If we extended the lines in both directions, they would never meet.

We show that two lines are parallel by drawing arrows on them like this:

Example 2.2 ▷ Two lines are perpendicular if the angle between them is 90°. This is also called a right angle.

90°

We show that two lines are perpendicular by labelling the 90° angle with a square corner.

1 Write down which of the following sets of lines are parallel.

a 　　b 　　c 　　d

e 　　f 　　g 　　h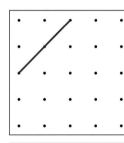

2 Copy each of the following diagrams onto square dotted paper.

On each diagram, use your ruler to draw two more lines that are parallel to the first line. Show that the lines are parallel by adding arrows to them.

a 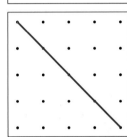　　b 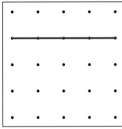　　c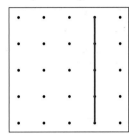

d 　　e 　　f

3 Write down which of the following pairs of lines are perpendicular.

a 　　b 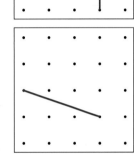　　c 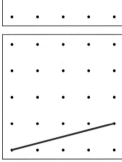　　d

e 　　f 　　g 　　h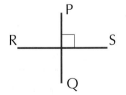

4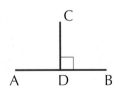

The line AB is perpendicular to the line CD.

Copy and complete the following.

a

The line XY is perpendicular to the line ......

b

The line ...... is perpendicular to the line ......

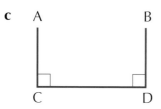

c The line CD is perpendicular to the lines ...... and ......

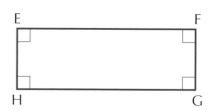

d The line ...... is perpendicular to the line .... The line EF is perpendicular to the lines ...... and ....

5 Copy each of the following diagrams onto square dotted paper. Add arrows and square corners to show which lines are perpendicular and which are parallel to each other.

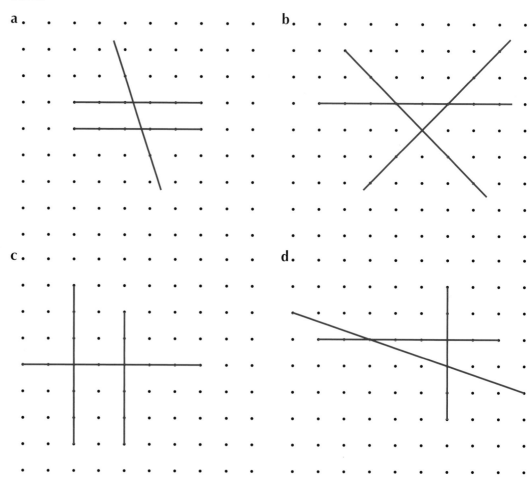

a.

b.

c.

d.

1   Draw sketches of at least five objects in your classroom that
  a   contain parallel lines
  b   contain perpendicular lines.
  Label any right angles on your sketches with square corners and any parallel lines with arrows.

2   Use your ruler to draw a straight line of any length.
  Now draw two more lines that are both perpendicular to this line.
  Write down what you notice about the two new lines.

Measuring and drawing angles

When two lines meet at a point, they form an **angle**. An angle is a measure of rotation and is measured in degrees (°).

Types of angle

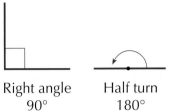

Right angle
90°

Half turn
180°

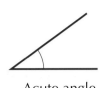

Full turn
360°

Acute angle
less than 90°

Obtuse angle
between 90° and 180°

Reflex angle
between 180° and 360°

Notice that on a semicircular protractor there are two scales. Both scales run from 0° to 180°. One goes clockwise and other goes anticlockwise. It is important that you use the correct scale.

When measuring or drawing an angle, always decide first whether it is an acute angle or an obtuse angle.

Example 2.3

First, decide whether the angle to be measured is acute or obtuse. This is an acute angle (less than 90°).

Place the centre of the protractor at the corner of the angle, as in the diagram.

The two angles shown on the protractor scales are 60° and 120°. Since you are measuring an acute angle, the angle is 60° (to the nearest degree).

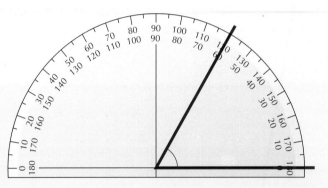

Example 2.4

Measure the size of this reflex angle.

First, measure the inside or interior angle. This is an obtuse angle.

The two angles shown on the protractor scales are 30° and 150°. Since you are measuring an obtuse angle, the angle is 150°.

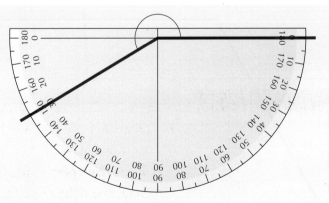

The size of the reflex angle is found by subtracting this angle from 360°. The reflex angle is therefore 360 – 150°, which is 210° (to the nearest degree).

1 Write down whether each of the following angles is acute, obtuse, reflex or a right angle.

a 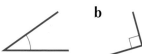 b c d e f g

2 Measure the size of each of the following angles, giving your answer to the nearest degree.

a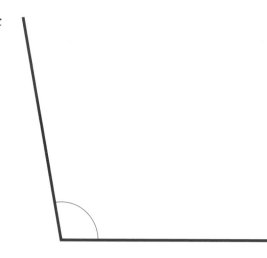

b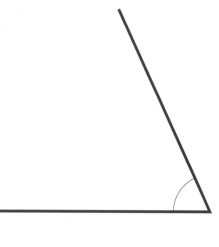

c

d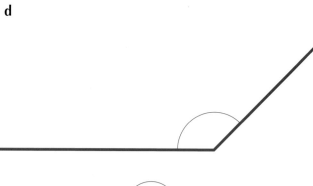

e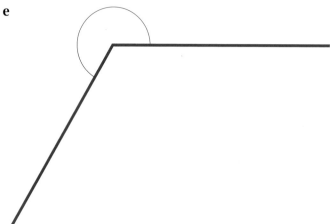

f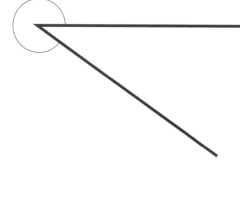

3 Draw and label each of the following angles.

a	30°	b	70°	c	45°	d	72°	e	120°
f	150°	g	95°	h	158°	i	290°	j	320°

Angles in a triangle

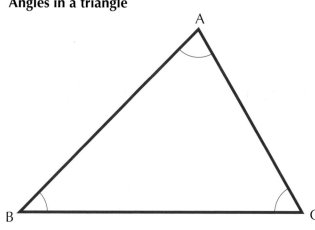

a   Measure the three angles in the triangle ABC.
Copy and complete the following:
Angle A = ...°, Angle B = ...°, Angle C = ...°

b   Add the three angles together.
Copy and complete the following:
Angle A + Angle B + Angle C = ...°

c   Now draw some triangles of your own and repeat the above.

d   Write down anything you notice.

Calculating angles

You can calculate the **unknown angles** in a diagram from the information given. Unknown angles are usually shown by letters, such as *a*, *b*, *c*, ...

Remember: usually the diagrams are not to scale.

Angles around a point

Angles around a point add up to 360°.

Example 2.5 ▷

Calculate the size of the angle *a*.

$a = 360° - 150° - 130°$
$a = 80°$

Angles on a straight line

Angles on a straight line add up to 180°.

Example 2.6 ▷

Calculate the size of the angle *b*.

$b = 180° - 155°$
$b = 25°$

Angles in a triangle   The angles in a triangle add up to 180°.

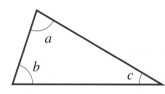

$a + b + c = 180°$

Example 2.7 ▷   Calculate the size of the angle c.

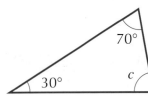

$$c = 180° - 70° - 30°$$
$$c = 80°$$

Vertically opposite angles   When two lines intersect, the opposite angles are equal.

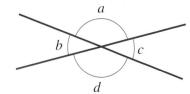

$a = d$ and $b = c$

Example 2.8 ▷   Calculate the sizes of angles d and e.

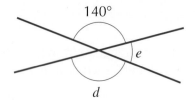

$d = 140°$ (opposite angles)

$e = 40°$ (angles on a straight line)

Exercise 2C

1 Calculate the size of each unknown angle.

a   **b**   **c**   **d**

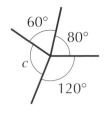

2 Calculate the size of each unknown angle.

a   **b**   **c**   **d**

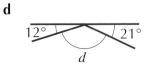

3 Calculate the size of each unknown angle.

a   **b**   **c**   **d**

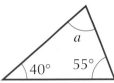 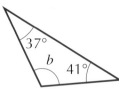

4 Calculate the size of each unknown angle.

a
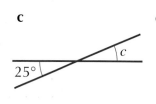

50°

b
138° X b

c
25° c

d
e d 37°

Extension Work

Calculate the size of the unknown angle in each diagram.

1
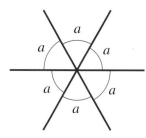
a a a
a a
a

2
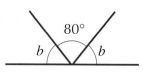
80°
b b

3
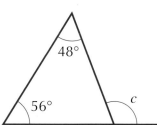
48°
56° c

4
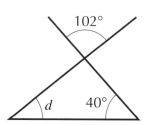
102°
d 40°

The geometric properties of quadrilaterals

Read carefully and learn all the properties of the quadrilaterals below.

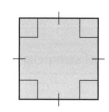

Square
- Four equal sides
- Four right angles
- Opposite sides parallel
- Diagonals bisect each other at right angles
- Four lines of symmetry
- Rotational symmetry of order four

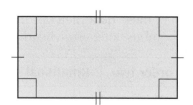

Rectangle
- Two pairs of equal sides
- Four right angles
- Opposite sides parallel
- Diagonals bisect each other
- Two lines of symmetry
- Rotational symmetry of order two

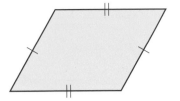

Parallelogram
- Two pairs of equal sides
- Two pairs of equal angles
- Opposite sides parallel
- Diagonals bisect each other
- No lines of symmetry
- Rotational symmetry of order two

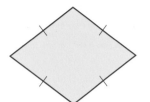

Rhombus
- Four equal sides
- Two pairs of equal angles
- Opposite sides parallel
- Diagonals bisect each other at right angles
- Two lines of symmetry
- Rotational symmetry of order two

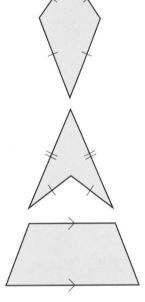

Kite
- Two pairs of adjacent sides of equal length
- One pair of equal angles
- Diagonals intersect at right angles
- One line of symmetry

Arrowhead or Delta
- Two pairs of adjacent sides of equal length
- One pair of equal angles
- Diagonals intersect at right angles outside the shape
- One line of symmetry

Trapezium
- One pair of parallel sides
- Some trapezia have one line of symmetry

Exercise 2D

① Copy the table below and put each of these quadrilaterals in the correct column: square, rectangle, parallelogram, rhombus, kite, arrowhead and trapezium.

No lines of symmetry	One line of symmetry	Two lines of symmetry	Fours lines of symmetry

② Copy the table below and put each of these quadrilaterals in the correct column: square, rectangle, parallelogram, rhombus, kite, arrowhead and trapezium.

Rotational symmetry of order one	Rotational symmetry of order two	Rotational symmetry of order four

3 A quadrilateral has four right angles and rotational symmetry of order two. What type of quadrilateral is it?

4 A quadrilateral has rotational symmetry of order two and no lines of symmetry. What type of quadrilateral is it?

5 Rachel says:

> A quadrilateral with four equal sides must be a square.

Is she right or wrong? Explain your answer.

6 Robert says:

> A quadrilateral with rotational symmetry of order two must be a rectangle

Is he right or wrong? Explain your answer.

7 A square is actually a special kind of rectangle. It is a rectangle with four equal sides. Complete the following sentences using the names of quadrilaterals:

   a A square is a special kind of …… and also a special kind of …….

   b A rectangle is a special kind of …….

   c A rhombus is a special kind of …….

Extension Work

The three-by-two rectangle below is to be cut into squares along its grid lines:

This can be done in two different ways:

and

Three squares   Six squares

Use squared paper to show the number of ways different sizes of rectangles can be cut into squares.

Constructions

The following two examples will remind you how to construct triangles with accurate measurements.

When constructing the triangles, you will need to be accurate enough to draw the lines to the nearest millimetre and the angles to the nearest degree.

You will need a sharp pencil, a ruler and a protractor.

Leave any construction lines and marks that you make on the completed diagram.

Example 2.9 ▷

Here is a sketch of a triangle ABC. It is not drawn accurately.

Construct the triangle ABC.
- Draw line BC 7 cm long.
- Draw an angle of 50° at B.
- Draw line AB 5 cm long.
- Join AC to complete the triangle.

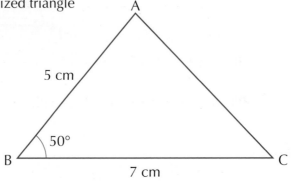

The completed, full-sized triangle is given on the right.

Example 2.10 ▷

Here is a sketch of a triangle XYZ. It is not drawn accurately.

Construct the triangle XYZ.
- Draw line YZ 8 cm long.
- Draw an angle of 40° at Y.
- Draw an angle of 50° at Z.
- Extend both angle lines to intersect at X to complete the triangle.

The completed, full-sized triangle is given on the right.

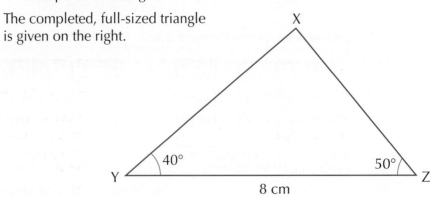

1. Construct each of the following triangles. Remember to label all lines and angles. The triangles are not drawn to scale.

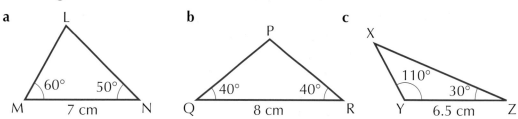

a
A
5 cm
40°
B   6 cm   C

b
D
5 cm   120°
E   8 cm   F

c
G
5.2 cm
H   4.8 cm   I

2. Construct each of the following triangles. Remember to label all lines and angles. The triangles are not drawn to scale.

a
L
60°   50°
M   7 cm   N

b
P
40°   40°
Q   8 cm   R

c
X
110°   30°
Y   6.5 cm   Z

3. Construct the triangle ABC with AB = 5 cm, angle A = 60° and angle B = 50°.

4. Construct the triangle XYZ with XY = 7 cm, XZ = 6 cm and angle X = 48°.

Extension Work

1. a Make an accurate copy of the parallelogram on the right.

   b Construct some accurate shapes of your own. First decide on the type of shape and draw a sketch of it. Label your sketch with the measurements you want your shape to have. Now make an accurate construction of the shape, using a ruler and protractor.

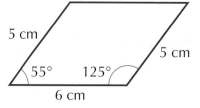

5 cm   5 cm
55°   125°
6 cm

2. Find out how to draw triangles using computer software packages such as LOGO.

What you need to know for level 4

- How to recognise the different types of angle
- The names of the different types of quadrilateral

What you need to know for level 5

- How to draw and measure angles to the nearest degree
- The angles of a triangle add up to 180°
- The symmetry properties of quadrilaterals
- How to construct triangles from given information

National Curriculum SATs questions

LEVEL 4

1 *2002 Paper 1*

Two pupils drew angles on square grids.

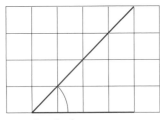

Angle A   Angle B

a Which word below describes angle A?

acute   obtuse   right-angled   reflex

b Is angle A bigger than angle B?

Explain your answer.

2 *1999 Paper 2*

a The time on this clock is 3 o'clock.

What is the size of the angle between the hands?

b Copy and complete this sentence, using a whole number.

At ... o'clock the size of the angle between the hands is 180°.

c What is the size of the angle between the hands at 1 o'clock?

d What is the size of the angle between the hands at 5 o'clock?

e How long does it take for the minute hand to move 360°?

LEVEL 5

3 *2000 Paper 1*

Look at these angles.

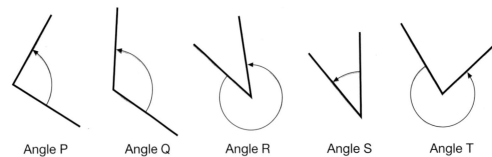

Angle P   Angle Q   Angle R   Angle S   Angle T

One of the angles measures 120°. Write its letter.

CHAPTER 3 Handling Data 1

This chapter is going to show you

- how to work with a probability scale
- how to work out probabilities in different situations
- how to use experimental probability to make predictions
- how to collect data from a simple experiment and record in a frequency table
- how to find probabilities based on equally likely outcomes

What you should already know

- Some basic ideas about chance and probability
- how to interpret data from line graphs, tables and bar charts

Probability

Look at the pictures. Which one is most likely to happen where you live today?

We use probability to decide how likely it is that different events will happen.

Example 3.1 　Here are some words we use when talking about whether something may happen:

very likely, unlikely, certain, impossible, an even chance, very unlikely, likely

The two complete opposites here are impossible and certain, with an even chance (evens) in the middle. So, these can be given in the order:

impossible, very unlikely, unlikely, **even chance**, likely, very likely, **certain**

Example 3.2 ▷ Four events, A, B, C and D, are shown on the probability scale.

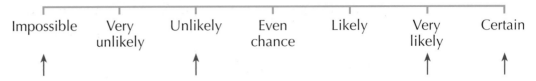

A is the probability that when a dice is rolled, the score is *not* 6.
B is the probability that when a dice is rolled, the score is either 1 or 2.
C is the probability that a coin will land to give either a Head or a Tail.
D is the probability that it will *not* rain at some time this year.

It is *very likely* that the dice will not give a score of 6.

There is less than an even chance that the dice will give a score of 1 or 2. So, it is unlikely.

The coin will land to give a Head or a Tail. So, it is *certain*.

It must rain at some time this year. So, not raining is *impossible*.

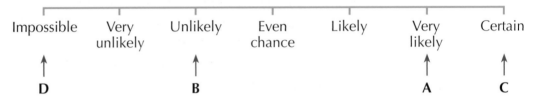

Example 3.3 ▷ Which is more likely to happen: Flipping the Tail on a coin or rolling a number less than 5 on a dice?

A coin can only land two ways (Head or Tail). So, provided the coin is fair, there is an even chance of landing on the Tail.

On a dice there are four numbers less than 5 and two numbers that are not. So, there is more than an even chance of rolling a number less than 5. So, rolling a number less than 5 is more likely than getting the Tail when a coin is flipped.

Example 3.4 ▷ A spinner has five equal sections.

What is the chance of the spinner landing on **a** 2 **b** 4 or 5?

a There is only one section with the number 2 on it.
So, it is very unlikely that the spinner will land on 2.

b There are two sections with 4 or 5 on them. So, there is less than an even chance of landing on 4 or 5, but this is twice as likely as landing on 2.

①

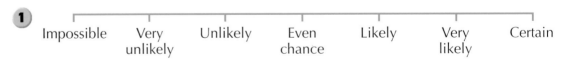

Copy the probability scale above. For each of the following events, write its letter **a**, **b**, **c**, **d** or **e** on the scale.

a Obtaining a Head when spinning a coin. **b** Winning the lottery with one ticket.
c It snowing in July in England. **d** The sun rising tomorrow.
e Rolling a dice and scoring more than 1.

2 Write down an event for which the outcome is:

    a certain   **b** impossible   **c** fifty-fifty chance   **d** very unlikely

    e likely   **f** very likely   **g** unlikely

3 Here are two grids:

Grid 1   Grid 2

A shape is picked at random. Copy and complete the sentences:

a Picking a triangle from Grid … is impossible.

b Picking a square from Grid … is likely.

c Picking a square from Grid … is unlikely.

d Picking a rectangle from Grid … is very unlikely.

e Picking a triangle from Grid … is fifty–fifty.

4 Bag A contains 2 red marbles, 1 blue marble and 1 green marble.   Bag A
A marble is picked at random.

Copy and complete each of these sentences.

a There is the same chance of picking a …… marble as a ……
marble.

b It is twice as likely that a …… marble is picked than a …… marble or a …….
marble.

Bag B contains 4 red marbles, 1 blue marble and no green marbles.   Bag B
A marble is picked at random.

Copy and complete each of these sentences.

c It is impossible to pick a …… marble.

d It is very likely that a …… marble is picked.

e From which bag is there a better chance of picking a blue marble? Explain your
answer.

5 A fair spinner has six sides, as shown. Copy and complete
each of these sentences.

a There is an even chance that the spinner will land on the
letter …

b It is unlikely that the spinner will land on the letter …

c It is very unlikely that the spinner will land on the letter…

6 A man has six blue shirts, three white shirts and one grey shirt in his wardrobe. He picks a shirt at random.

Copy and complete each of these sentences.
  a It is likely that the man will pick a …… shirt.
  b It is twice as likely that the man will pick a …… shirt than a …… shirt.
  c It is very unlikely that the man will pick a …… shirt
  d It is …… that the man will pick a green shirt.

Probability scales

The probability of an event is:

$$P(\text{event}) = \frac{\text{Number of outcomes in the event}}{\text{Total number of all possible outcomes}}$$

Probabilities can be written as either fractions or decimals. They always take values between 0 and 1, including 0 and 1. The probability of an event happening can be shown on the probability scale:

```
┌───┬───┬───┬───┬───┬───┬───┬───┬───┬───┐
0   0.1 0.2 0.3 0.4 0.5 0.6 0.7 0.8 0.9  1
Impossible          Even chance          Certain
```

If an event is the complete opposite of another event, such as raining and not raining, then their probabilities add up to 1.

Look at the probability scale and see how many pairs of decimals you can find that add up to 1.

Example 3.5 ▷   There are ten coloured counters in a bag. Three are blue, five are red and the rest are yellow. A counter is picked out at random. Calculate the probability of the counter being:

  a blue   **b** red   **c** yellow

  a As there are 3 blue counters out of 10 counters altogether, the probability of getting a blue counter is $\frac{3}{10}$

  b As there are 5 red counters out of 10 counters altogether, the probability of getting a red counter is $\frac{5}{10} = \frac{1}{2}$

  c As there are 2 yellow counters out of 10 counters altogether, the probability of getting a yellow counter is $\frac{2}{10} = \frac{1}{5}$.

Example 3.6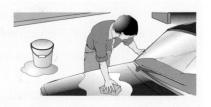

The probability that a woman washes her car on Sunday is 0.7. What is the probability that she does not wash her car?

These two events are opposites of each other, so the probabilities add up to 1. The probability that she does not wash her car is $1 - 0.7 = 0.3$.

Example 3.7

A girl plays a game of tennis. The probability that she wins is $\frac{2}{3}$. What is the probability that she loses?

Probability of not winning (losing) $= 1 - \frac{2}{3}$

$= \frac{1}{3}$

Example 3.8

Here are the probabilities of different events happening. What are the probabilities of these events not happening?

a 0.4   **b** 0.8   **c** 0.75   **d** 0.16   **e** $\frac{1}{4}$ **f** $\frac{3}{5}$ **g** $\frac{3}{8}$

The probabilities of the events not happening are:

a $1 - 0.4 = 0.6$ **b** $1 - 0.8 = 0.2$ **c** $1 - 0.75 = 0.25$

d $1 - 0.16 = 0.84$ **e** $1 - \frac{1}{4} = \frac{3}{4}$ **f** $1 - \frac{3}{5} = \frac{2}{5}$ **g** $1 - \frac{3}{8} = \frac{5}{8}$

Exercise 3B

1 Here is a probability scale:

The probability of events A, B, C and D happening are shown on the scale. Copy the scale and mark on it the probabilities of A, B, C and D not happening. For example, write 'Not B' on scale.

2 Copy and complete the table.

Event	Probability of event occurring (p)	Probability of event not occurring ($1 - p$)
A	0.2	
B	0.3	
C	0.6	
D	1	
E	$\frac{1}{4}$	
F	$\frac{1}{3}$	
G	$\frac{3}{4}$	

3 Ten cards are numbered 0 to 9.   0 1 2 3 4 5 6 7 8 9

A card is picked at random. Work out the probability that it is

a 2   **b** not 2   **c** odd   **d** not odd

e 7, 8 or 9   **f** less than 7   **g** 4 or 5   **h** not 4 or 5

4 In a bus station there are 24 red buses, 6 blue buses and 10 green buses. Calculate the probability that the next bus to arrive is:

a green **b** red **c** red or blue **d** yellow **e** not green

f not red **g** neither red nor blue **h** not yellow

5 A bag contains 32 counters that are either black or white. The probability that a counter is black is $\frac{1}{4}$.

a What is the probability that the counter is white?

b How many black counters are in the bag?

c How many white counters are in the bag?

Extension Work

Design a spreadsheet to convert the probabilities of events happening into the probabilities that they do not happen.

Collecting data for a frequency table

Handling data is about collecting and organising data. It is also about presenting data using diagrams and being able to interpret diagrams.

Example 3.9

A spinner has five different coloured sections on it: red, green, blue, yellow and black. You want to test whether the spinner is fair by recording which colour the spinner lands on each time you spin it. Here is a table in which to record the results each time the spinner is spun. Each result is recorded with a tick.

Trial number	Red	Green	Blue	Yellow	Black
1					✓
2	✓				
3	✓				
4			✓		
5				✓	
6			✓		
7	✓				
8					✓
9				✓	
10					✓
Total	3	0	2	2	3

One conclusion from these results is that the spinner might be biased (not fair), because it never landed on green.

To be more certain, you would need to carry out many more trials – 50 spins at least!

Example 3.10 ▷ Use the results in Example 3.9 to estimate the probability of the spinner

    a   landing on red   **b**   landing on green   **c**   landing on blue
    d   landing on yellow   **e**   landing on black.

    a   There are 3 reds out of 10, so the estimate of $P(\text{red}) = \frac{3}{10}$
    b   There are no reds out of 10 so the estimate of $P(\text{green}) = 0$

Similarly for blue, yellow and black:

    c $P(\text{blue}) = \frac{2}{10} = \frac{1}{5}$ **d** $P(\text{yellow}) = \frac{2}{10} = \frac{1}{5}$ **e** $P(\text{black}) = \frac{3}{10}$

Exercise 3C

1 Make your own spinner from a piece of card. It can have five sections, as in Example 3.9, or a different number of sections. Label the sections with numbers or each in a different colour. Spin the spinner 50 times and record the results in a table. Comment on whether you think that your spinner is biased.

2 Put 20 coloured counters in a bag. Now draw out a counter, note the colour and replace it. Repeat this 50 times. Record the results in a tally chart. Use your results to estimate the probability of choosing each colour. Check your results by emptying the bag.

3 Roll a dice 60 times. Record the results in a table. Use the results to estimate the probability of each score. Comment on whether you think the dice is biased.

Extension Work

Collect data on the results of ten recent Premiership football matches. Use the results to predict the number of home wins, away wins and draws in ten matches next week. Check the results to see how accurate your predictions were.

Events

Look at the pictures of the yachts. Can you spot the differences? Some yachts have a flag on the top of the mainmast. The sails and hulls are different colours.

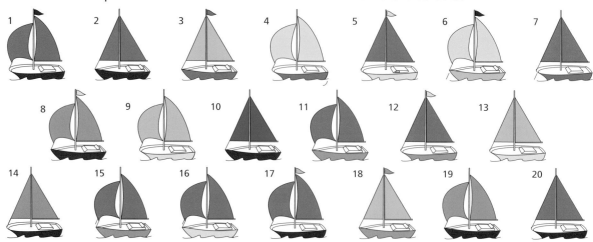

Look at the 20 yachts in the picture and answer the questions.

1 How many yachts have each of these features?

 a   Round sails   **b**   A blue hull   **c**   Yellow sails

 d   A flag at the top of the mainmast   **e**   A pointed hull

 f   Red sails and a curved hull   **g**   A yellow hull but no flag

 h   Straight green sails   **i**   A curved red hull

 j   A red hull, blue sails and a flag at the top of the mainmast

2 A sailor takes a yacht at random. What is the probability that it has each of the following?

 a   Round sails   **b**   A blue hull   **c**   Yellow sails

 d   A flag at the top of the mainmast   **e**   A pointed hull

 f   Red sails and a curved hull   **g**   A yellow hull but no flag

 h   Straight green sails   **i**   A curved red hull

 j   A red hull, blue sails and a flag at the top of the mainmast

3 Here is a list of events for the 20 yachts.

Event A: A yacht has a blue hull.
Event B: A yacht has round sails.
Event C: A yacht has a flag at the top of the mainmast.
Event D: A yacht has a green hull.
Event E: A yacht has straight sails.
Event F: A yacht has red sails and a red hull.
Event G: A yacht has a pointed blue hull.
Event H: A yacht has a straight green sail.

Which of these events can be true at the same time?

a A and B	**b** A and C	**c** A and D	**d** A and E
e A and G	**f** A and H	**g** B and E	**h** B and F
i B and G	**j** B and H	**k** C and F	**l** C and H
m D and E	**n** E and F	**o** F and G	**p** F and H

Work out how many different types of yacht there are altogether if there is a choice of round sails or straight sails, sail colour (red, blue, green or yellow), flag at the top of the mainmast, or no flag, curved hull or pointed hull, and colour of hull (red, blue, green or yellow).

Extend the problem by changing the colour of the flag or by adding other features to the yachts.

Experimental probability

Will the train be late again today?

Look at the picture. How could you estimate the probability that a train will be late?

You could keep a record of the number of times that the train arrives late over a period of 10 days. Then use these results to estimate the probability that it will be late in future.

$$\text{Experimental probability} = \frac{\text{Number of events in trials}}{\text{Total number of trials carried out}}$$

Example 3.11 ▷ An electrician wants to estimate the probability that a new light bulb lasts for less than 1 month. He fits 20 new bulbs and 3 of them failed within 1 month. What is his estimate of the probability that a new light bulb will fail?

3 out of 20 bulbs failed within 1 month. So the experimental probability $= \frac{3}{20}$

Example 3.12 ▷ A dentist keeps a record of the number of fillings she gives her patients over 2 weeks. Here are her results:

Number of fillings	None	1	More than 1
Number of patients	80	54	16

Estimate the probability that a patient does not need a filling (there are 150 records altogether).

$$\text{Experimental probability} = \frac{80}{150}$$
$$= \frac{8}{15}$$

Example 3.13 ▷ A company manufactures items for computers. The number of faulty items is recorded:

Number of items produced	Number of faulty items	Experimental probability
100	8	0.08
200	20	
500	45	
1000	82	

a Copy and complete the table.

b Which is the best estimate of the probability of an item being faulty? Explain your answer.

a

Number of items produced	Number of faulty items	Experimental probability
100	8	0.08
200	20	$20 \div 200 = 0.1$
500	45	$45 \div 500 = 0.09$
1000	82	$82 \div 1000 = 0.082$

b The last result (0.082), as the experiment is based on more results.

Exercise 3E

1 A boy decides to carry out an experiment to estimate the probability of a drawing pin landing with the pin pointing up. He drops 50 drawing pins and records the result. He then repeats the experiment several times. Here are his results:

Number of drawing pins	Number pointing up
50	32
100	72
150	106
200	139
250	175

a From the results, would you say that there is a greater chance of a drawing pin landing point up or point down? Explain your answer.

b Which result is the most reliable and why?

c Estimate the probability of a drawing pin landing point up.

d How could the boy improve the experiment?

2 A girl wishes to test whether a dice is biased. She rolls the dice 60 times. The results are shown in the table:

Score	1	2	3	4	5	6
Frequency	6	12	10	9	15	8

a Do you think the dice is biased? Give a reason for your answer.

b How could she improve the experiment?

c From the results, estimate the probability of rolling 1.

d From the results, estimate the probability of rolling 1 or 4.

3 The number of winning raffle tickets sold in a charity event is recorded.

a Copy and complete the table:

Number of tickets sold	Number of winning tickets	Experimental probability
50	7	$\frac{7}{50} = 0.14$
100	15	
200	32	
500	75	

b Which experimental probability is the most reliable? Give a reason for your answer.

Extension Work

Decide on an experiment of your own. Write down a report of how you would carry it out and how you would record your results.

What you need to know for level 4

○ How to collect data using a frequency table
○ How to read and interpret data from line graphs, bar charts and tables

What you need to know for level 5

○ How to use a probability scale from 0 to 1
○ How to find and justify probabilities based on equally likely outcomes and experimental evidence
○ To understand that different outcomes may result from repeating an experiment

National Curriculum SATs questions

LEVEL 4

1 *1996 Paper 2*

A machine sells sweets in five different colours:

red   green   orange   yellow   purple

You cannot choose which colour you get.

There is the same number of each colour in the machine.

Two boys want to buy a sweet each.

I don't like yellow ones or orange ones.

Ken

I like all of them.

Colin

a What is the probability that Ken will get a sweet that he likes?

b What is the probability that Colin will get a sweet that he likes?

c Draw an arrow on the scale to show the probability that Ken will get a sweet that he likes.

0   1

d Draw an arrow on the scale to show the probability that Colin will get a sweet that he likes.

0   1

e Mandy buys one sweet. The arrow on this scale shows the probability that Mandy gets a sweet that she likes.

Mandy

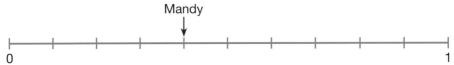

0   1

Write a sentence that could describe which sweets Mandy likes.

2 *1997 Paper 2*

a Joe has these cards:

Sara takes a card without looking.

Joe says:

On Sara's card, ■ is more likely than △

Explain why Joe is wrong.

Here are some words and phrases:

impossible	not likely	certain	likely

Choose a word or phrase to fill in the gaps below.

It is …… that the number on Sara's card will be smaller than 10.

It is …… that the number on Sara's card will be an odd number.

b Joe still has these cards:

He mixes them up and puts them face down on the table. Then he turns the first card over, like this:

Joe is going to turn over the next card.

Copy and complete this sentence:

On the next card, …… is less likely than ……

Is the number on the next card likely to be higher than 5 or lower than 5, or is it not possible to say?

Explain your answer.

LEVEL 5

3   *1999 Paper 1*

A coin has two sides, heads and tails.

a   Chris is going to toss a coin.

What is the probability that Chris will get heads? Write your answer as a fraction.

b   Sion is going to toss two coins.

Complete a table of two columns to show the different results he could get.

c   Sion is going to toss two coins.

What is the probability that he will get tails with both his coins? Write your answer as a fraction.

d   Dianne tossed one coin.

She got tails.

Dianne is going to toss another coin.

What is the probability that she will get tails again with her next coin? Write your answer as a fraction.

4   2000 Paper 2

In each box of cereal there is a free gift of a card.

You cannot tell which card will be in a box. Each card is equally likely.

There are four different cards: A, B, C or D

a   Zoe needs card A.

Her brother Paul needs cards C and D.

They buy one box of cereal.

What is the probability that the card is one that Zoe needs?

What is the probability that the card is one that Paul needs?

b   Then their mother opens the box. She tells them the card is not card A.

Now what is the probability the card is one that Zoe needs?

What is the probability that the card is one that Paul needs?

CHAPTER 4

Number **2**

This chapter is going to show you	What you should already know
○ more about working with fractions, decimals and percentages ○ how to calculate simple percentages of quantities ○ how to add and subtract fractions with a common denominator	○ The equivalences of common fractions, decimals and percentages ○ How to add and subtract fractions with denominators 2, 4 and 8 ○ How to calculate ten per cent of a quantity

Fractions and decimals

These diagrams show shapes with various fractions of them shaded. Can you write each of them as a decimal, a fraction and a percentage?

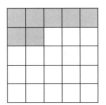 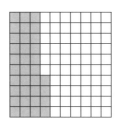 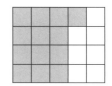 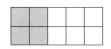

Example 4.1

Cancel each of the following fractions to its simplest form.

a $\frac{20}{50}$ **b** $\frac{12}{16}$ **c** $\frac{4}{28}$

a $\frac{20}{50} = \frac{2}{5}$ (Cancel by 10.)

b $\frac{12}{16} = \frac{3}{4}$ (Cancel by 4.)

c $\frac{4}{28} = \frac{1}{7}$ (Cancel by 4.)

Example 4.2

Work out the each of these decimals as a fraction.

a   0.6   **b**   0.45

a $0.6 = \frac{60}{100} = \frac{3}{5}$ (Cancel by 20.)   **b** $0.45 = \frac{45}{100} = \frac{9}{20}$ (Cancel by 5.)

Exercise 4A

1 Cancel each of these fractions to its simplest form.

a $\frac{4}{12}$ **b** $\frac{6}{9}$ **c** $\frac{14}{21}$ **d** $\frac{15}{20}$ **e** $\frac{18}{20}$ **f** $\frac{20}{50}$

g $\frac{8}{24}$ **h** $\frac{6}{12}$ **i** $\frac{4}{24}$ **j** $\frac{12}{20}$ **k** $\frac{16}{24}$ **l** $\frac{25}{35}$

2 Write each of the following decimals as a fraction with a denominator of 10. Then cancel the fraction to its simplest form, if possible.

a	0.2	**b**	0.4	**c**	0.1	**d**	0.3
e	0.6	**f**	0.9	**g**	0.5	**h**	0.8

3 Write each of the following decimals as a fraction with a denominator of 100. Then cancel the fraction to its simplest form, if possible.

a	0.25	**b**	0.45	**c**	0.12	**d**	0.38
e	0.66	**f**	0.95	**g**	0.52	**h**	0.84
i	0.28	**j**	0.65	**k**	0.98	**l**	0.36
m	0.05	**n**	0.06	**o**	0.48	**p**	0.15

4 Using your answers to questions 2 and 3 write down the decimal equivalent to each of these fractions.

a $\frac{3}{5}$ **b** $\frac{3}{20}$ **c** $\frac{3}{25}$ **d** $\frac{3}{50}$

5 Write down each of the following terminating decimals.

a $\frac{1}{2}$ **b** $\frac{1}{4}$ **c** $\frac{1}{5}$ **d** $\frac{1}{10}$ **e** $\frac{1}{20}$ **f** $\frac{1}{25}$ **g** $\frac{1}{50}$ **h** $\frac{1}{100}$

By dividing the numerator by the denominator, work out the ninths as recurring decimals. They are:

$$\frac{1}{9} \quad \frac{2}{9} \quad \frac{3}{9} \quad \frac{4}{9} \quad \frac{5}{9} \quad \frac{6}{9} \quad \frac{7}{9} \quad \frac{8}{9}$$

Describe any patterns that you can see in the digits.

Adding and subtracting fractions

All of the grids below contain 100 squares. Some of the squares have been shaded in. The fraction shaded is shown in its lowest terms.
Use the diagrams to work out $1 - (\frac{1}{5} + \frac{7}{20} + \frac{22}{50} + \frac{1}{25})$.

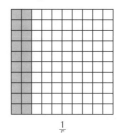 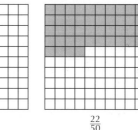

$\frac{1}{5}$ $\frac{7}{20}$ $\frac{22}{50}$ $\frac{1}{25}$

Example 4.3

Add together:

a $\frac{1}{5} + \frac{2}{5}$ **b** $\frac{3}{8} + \frac{1}{8}$ **c** $\frac{1}{3} + \frac{1}{3} + \frac{2}{3}$

a In each addition, the denominators are the same. So, the numerators are just added. $\frac{1}{5} + \frac{2}{5} = \frac{3}{5}$

b $\frac{3}{8} + \frac{1}{8} = \frac{4}{8} = \frac{1}{2}$ Note: the answer here has been cancelled.

c $\frac{1}{3} + \frac{1}{3} + \frac{2}{3} = \frac{4}{3} = 1\frac{1}{3}$ Note: this answer is a top-heavy fraction. So, it should be written as a mixed number.

43

Example 4.4 Subtract:

a $\frac{5}{6} - \frac{1}{6}$ b $\frac{5}{8} - \frac{3}{8}$.

a In each subtraction, the denominators are the same. So, the numerators are just subtracted. $\frac{5}{6} - \frac{1}{6} = \frac{4}{6} = \frac{2}{3}$

b $\frac{5}{8} - \frac{3}{8} = \frac{2}{8} = \frac{1}{4}$.

Note that both of these answers can be cancelled.

Example 4.5 Work out:

a $\frac{3}{4}$ of £28   b $5 \times \frac{2}{3}$

a $\frac{1}{4}$ of £28 = £7. So $\frac{3}{4}$ of £28 = 3 × £7 = £21

b $5 \times \frac{2}{3} = \frac{10}{3} = 3\frac{1}{3}$

Exercise 4B

1 Add each of the following pairs of fractions. Cancel or write as a mixed number as necessary.

a $\frac{1}{3} + \frac{1}{3}$ b $\frac{2}{5} + \frac{1}{5}$ c $\frac{1}{7} + \frac{2}{7}$ d $\frac{1}{4} + \frac{1}{4}$

e $\frac{1}{5} + \frac{3}{5}$ f $\frac{3}{8} + \frac{3}{8}$ g $\frac{5}{6} + \frac{5}{6}$ h $\frac{3}{4} + \frac{3}{4}$

2 Subtract each of the following pairs of fractions. Cancel as necessary.

a $\frac{2}{3} - \frac{1}{3}$ b $\frac{2}{5} - \frac{1}{5}$ c $\frac{2}{7} - \frac{1}{7}$ d $\frac{3}{4} - \frac{1}{4}$

e $\frac{3}{5} - \frac{1}{5}$ f $\frac{5}{8} - \frac{1}{8}$ g $\frac{5}{6} - \frac{1}{6}$ h $\frac{5}{9} - \frac{2}{9}$

3 Work out each of the following, cancelling down or writing as a mixed number as appropriate.

a $\frac{2}{3} + \frac{2}{3}$ b $\frac{5}{8} + \frac{7}{8}$ c $\frac{3}{10} + \frac{1}{10}$ d $\frac{1}{8} + \frac{5}{8}$

e $\frac{4}{15} + \frac{2}{15}$ f $\frac{7}{16} + \frac{1}{16}$ g $\frac{7}{12} + \frac{1}{12}$ h $\frac{3}{4} + \frac{1}{4} + \frac{1}{4}$

i $\frac{7}{8} - \frac{1}{8}$ j $\frac{5}{12} - \frac{1}{12}$ k $\frac{3}{10} - \frac{1}{10}$ l $\frac{8}{9} - \frac{1}{9}$

m $\frac{4}{15} - \frac{1}{15}$ n $\frac{7}{8} - \frac{5}{8}$ o $\frac{7}{12} - \frac{1}{12}$ p $\frac{3}{4} + \frac{3}{4} - \frac{1}{4}$

4 Work out each of these.

a $\frac{5}{8}$ of £32   b $\frac{3}{16}$ of 64 kg   c $\frac{2}{3}$ of £45   d $\frac{5}{6}$ of 240 cm

e $\frac{5}{9}$ of £45   f $\frac{2}{7}$ of £28   g $\frac{2}{9}$ of £90   h $\frac{2}{11}$ of 22 m

5 Work out each of these, cancelling down or writing as a mixed number as appropriate.

a $5 \times \frac{3}{4}$ b $7 \times \frac{4}{5}$ c $9 \times \frac{2}{3}$ d $4 \times \frac{7}{8}$

e $\frac{3}{8} \times 2$ f $\frac{7}{8} \times 8$ g $\frac{2}{3} \times 6$ h $\frac{5}{9} \times 3$

Extension Work

Copy the diagram on the right.
Shade in, in separate parts of the diagram, each of these fractions: $\frac{1}{12}, \frac{5}{24}, \frac{1}{8}, \frac{1}{4}, \frac{1}{6}$.

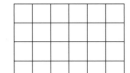

Write down the answer to

$1 - (\frac{1}{12} + \frac{5}{24} + \frac{1}{8} + \frac{1}{4} + \frac{1}{6})$

Put your answer in its simplest form.

Percentages

Example 4.6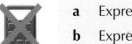

Without using a calculator:

a Express 8 as a percentage of 25.

b Express 39 as a percentage of 50.

a Write as a fraction: $\frac{8}{25}$. Multiply top and bottom by 4 to get $\frac{32}{100}$. So, 8 is 32% of 25.

b Write as a fraction: $\frac{39}{50}$. Multiply top and bottom by 2 to get $\frac{78}{100}$. So, 39 is 78% of 50.

Example 4.7

Find each of the following.

a What percentage of 10 is 8?   **b** What percentage of 20 is 14?

a Write as a fraction: $\frac{8}{10}$. Convert to a percentage by multiplying top and bottom by 10 to get 80%.

b Write as a fraction: $\frac{14}{20}$. Convert to a percentage by multiplying top and bottom by 5 to get 70%.

Example 4.8

Ashram scored 38 out of 50 in a Physics test, 16 out of 20 in a Chemistry test and 18 out of 25 in a Biology test. In which science did he do best?

Convert each mark to a percentage:

Physics: $\frac{38}{50} = \frac{76}{100} = 76\%$

Chemistry: $\frac{16}{20} = \frac{80}{100} = 80\%$

Biology: $\frac{18}{25} = \frac{72}{100} = 72\%$

So Chemistry was Ashram's best mark.

Exercise 4C

1 Write each of the following fractions as percentages.

a $\frac{1}{2}$ **b** $\frac{1}{4}$ **c** $\frac{3}{4}$ **d** $\frac{1}{10}$

e $\frac{1}{5}$ **f** $\frac{2}{25}$ **g** $\frac{7}{20}$ **h** $\frac{1}{25}$

2 Without using a calculator express the first quantity as a percentage of the second.

a 32 out of 50   **b** 17 out of 20   **c** 24 out of 50   **d** 16 out of 25

e 12 out of 20   **f** 3 out of 10   **g** 64 out of 100 **h** 18 out of 25

i 33 out of 50   **j** 18 out of 50   **k** 2 out of 25   **l** 6 out of 25

m 13 out of 20   **n** 34 out of 50   **o** 15 out of 50   **p** 48 out of 100

3 In the SATs test, Trevor scored 39 out of 50 in Maths, 16 out of 20 in English and 19 out of 25 in Science. Convert each of these scores to a percentage. In which test did Trevor do best?

4 Mr Wilson pays £50 a month to cover his electricity, gas and oil bills. Electricity costs £24. Gas costs £18 and the rest is for oil. What percentage of the total does each fuel cost?

5 My phone bill last month was £50. Of this, I spent £13 on Internet calls, £24 on long-distance calls and the rest on local calls. What percentage of the bill did I spend on each of type of call?

Extension **Work**

34 out of 200 is the same as 17 out of 100 (cancelling by 2), which is 17%.

Work out each of the following as percentages.

a 122 out of 200   **b** 93 out of 300   **c** 640 out of 1000
d 44 out of 400   **e** 60 out of 200   **f** 320 out of 400

Percentage increase and decrease

SPORTY SHOES
$\frac{1}{3}$ off all trainers

SHOES-FOR-YOU
30% off all trainers

Which shop gives the best value?

Example 4.9

a A clothes shop has a sale and reduces its prices by 20%. How much is the sale price of each of the following?

    i A jacket originally costing £45.   **ii** A dress originally costing £125.

    i 20% of 45 is 2 × 10% of 45 = 2 × 4.5 = 9. So, the jacket costs £45 – £9 = £36.

    ii 20% of 125 is 2 × 10% of 125 = 2 × 12.50 = 25. So, the dress costs £125 – £25 = £100.

b A company gives all its workers a 5% pay rise. What is the new wage of:

    i Joan, who originally earned £240 per week?

    ii Jack, who originally earned £6.00 per hour?

    i 5% of 240 is $\frac{1}{2}$ × 10% of 240 = $\frac{1}{2}$ × 24 = 12. So, Joan now earns £240 + £12 = £252 per week.

    ii 5% of 6.00 is $\frac{1}{2}$ × 10% of 6.00 = $\frac{1}{2}$ × 60p = 30p. So, Jack now earns £6.00 + 30p = £6.30 per hour.

Do not use a calculator for these questions.

1 A bat colony has 40 bats. Over the breeding season, the population increases by 30%.

    a How many new bats were born?

    b How many bats are there in the colony after the breeding season?

2 In a wood there are 20 000 midges. During the evening, bats eat 40% of the midges.

    a How many midges were eaten by the bats?

    b How many midges were left after the bats had eaten?

    c What percentage of midges remain?

3 Work out the final amount when:

    a £45 is increased by 10%   **b** £48 is decreased by 10%

    c £120 is increased by 20%   **d** £90 is decreased by 20%

    e £65 is increased by 15%   **f** £110 is decreased by 15%

    g £250 is increased by 25%   **h** £300 is decreased by 20%

    i £6.80 is increased by 10%   **j** £5.40 is decreased by 10%

4 **a** In a sale, all prices are reduced by 15%. Give the new price of an item that previously cost:

        i £18   **ii** £26   **iii** £50   **iv** £70

    b An electrical company increases its prices by 5%. Give the new price of an item that previously cost:

        i £200   **ii** £130   **iii** £380   **iv** £100

Extension Work

The government charges us VAT at $17\frac{1}{2}$% on most things we buy. Although this seems like an awkward percentage to work out, there is an easy way to do it without a calculator! It is easy to find 10%, which can be used to find 5% (divide the 10% value by 2). This can in turn be used to find $2\frac{1}{2}$% (divide the 5% value by 2). Adding together these three values gives 10% + 5% + $2\frac{1}{2}$% = $17\frac{1}{2}$%.

For example, find the VAT on an item that costs £24 before VAT is added.

10% of £24 = £2.40, 5% of £24 is £1.20, and $2\frac{1}{2}$% of £24 is £0.60.

So, $17\frac{1}{2}$% of £24 = £2.40 + £1.20 + £0.60 = £4.20.

Work out the VAT on an item that costs:

  a £30   **b** £40   **c** £50   **d** £90   **e** £120   **f** £200

Real-life problems

Percentages occur everyday in many situations. You have already met percentage increase and decrease. Three other examples are buying goods on credit, profit/loss and paying tax.

Example 4.10 ▷ A car costing £6000 can be bought on credit by paying a 25% deposit and followed by 24 monthly payments of £200.

    a   How much will the car cost on credit?

    b   What is the extra cost above the usual price?

    a   Deposit: 25% of £6000 = £1500. Payments: 24 × £200 = £4800.
        Total paid = £1500 + £4800 = £6300.

    b   Extra cost = £6300 – £6000 = £300.

Example 4.11 ▷ A jeweller makes a brooch for £200 and sells it for £250. What is the percentage profit?

    The profit is £250 – £200 = £50. £50 is one quarter of £200, which is 25%.

Exercise 4E

1. A mountain bike that normally costs £480 can be bought using three different plans:

Plan	Deposit	Number of payments	Each payment
A	20%	24	£22
B	50%	12	£20
C	10%	36	£18

    a   Work out how much the bike costs using each plan.

    b   Work out the extra cost of each plan.

2. A shop buys a radio for £50 and sells it for £60. Work out the percentage profit made by the shop.

3. A CD costs £14. The shop paid £10 for it. What is the percentage profit?

4. A car that costs £7000 can be bought by paying a 20% deposit, followed by 24 monthly payments of £200 and a final payment of £2000.

    a   How much will the car cost using the credit scheme?

    b   What is the extra cost of the credit scheme?

5. A shop sells a toaster for £20 in a sale. It cost the shop £25. What is the percentage loss?

6 An insurance policy for a motorbike is £300. It can be paid for by a 25% deposit followed by five payments of £50.

    a   How much does the policy cost using the scheme?

    b   What the extra cost of using the scheme?

7 Which of these schemes is cheaper to buy a three-piece suite worth £1000?

    Scheme A: No deposit followed by 25 payments of £50.

    Scheme B: 25% deposit followed by 25 payments of £30.

    Give a reason why someone might prefer scheme A.

What you need to know for level 4

- How to recognise simple fractions and their decimal and percentage equivalents
- Understand what per cent means
- How to add and subtract simple fractions and those with the same denominator

What you need to know for level 5

- Equivalent fractions, decimals and percentages for a wider range and how to convert between them.
- How to calculate simple percentages.
- How to calculate simple fractions of quantities and how to multiply a fraction by an integer.

National Curriculum SATs questions

LEVEL 4

1 *1997 Paper 1*

Diagram A

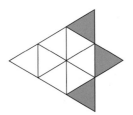
Diagram B

Diagram C

$\frac{1}{2}$ of diagram A is shaded.

    a   What fraction of shape B is shaded? What percentage of shape B is shaded?

    b   Copy and shade $\frac{2}{5}$ of shape C. What percentage of shape C have you shaded?

2 *2001 Paper 1*

    a Look at these fractions: $\frac{1}{2}$ $\frac{1}{3}$ $\frac{5}{6}$

       Mark each fraction on the number line.

       The first one has been done for you.

    b Fill in the numbers missing from the boxes.

$$\frac{2}{12} = \frac{\square}{6} \qquad\qquad \frac{1}{2} = \frac{2}{\square} \qquad\qquad \frac{12}{\square} = \frac{6}{24}$$

LEVEL 5

3 *1998 Paper 1*

This is how Caryl works out 15% of 120 in her head.

    a Show how Caryl can work out $17\frac{1}{2}$% of 240 in her head.

    b Work out 35% of 520. Show your working.

10% of 120 is 12
5% of 120 is 6
so 15% of 120 is 18

4 *2001 Paper 1*

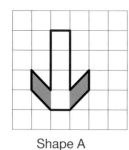 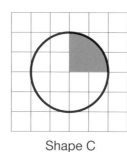 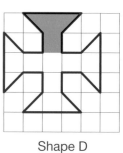

    Shape A   Shape B   Shape C   Shape D

    a What fraction of shape A is shaded?

    b What percentage of shape B is shaded?

    c Which of shape C or shape D has the greater percentage shaded?

       Explain how you know.

This chapter is going to show you

- how to simplify expressions
- how to expand brackets
- how to use index notation

What you should already know

- How to substitute into algebraic expressions
- How to add, subtract and multiply with negative numbers

Algebraic shorthand

In algebra, avoid using the $\times$ sign whenever you can, because it is easily confused with the variable x. Use instead the shorthand form of multiplication. For example:

$3m$ for $3 \times m$ ab for $a \times b$ $4cd$ for $d \times 4c$

Also, the $\div$ sign is often not used. So, for example:

$\frac{a}{b}$ is written instead of $a \div b$

Use of the equals sign

Each side of the = sign must have the same value. The two sides may look different, but are still equal.

Example 5.1 ▷ Which of the following expressions are equal to each other?

$$2 + 3 \qquad 4 \times 3 \qquad 5 - 2 \qquad 3 + 2 \qquad a + b \qquad b - a \qquad ab \qquad \frac{b}{c} \qquad bc$$

$$\frac{a}{b} \qquad b + a \qquad a - b \qquad 3 \times 4 \qquad 3 + 3 \qquad 10 \div 2 \qquad 2 \div 10 \qquad 2 - 5$$

Write correct mathematical statements for those that are equal.

$2 + 3$ is the same as $3 + 2$. That is: $2 + 3 = 3 + 2$

4×3 is the same as 3×4. That is: $4 \times 3 = 3 \times 4$

$a + b$ is the same as $b + a$. That is: $a + b = b + a$

ab is the same as ba. That is: $ab = ba$

None of the others are the same.

Example 5.2 ▷ Solve the equation $x + 2 = 7$.

What do you add to 2 to get 7?

You know that $5 + 2 = 7$

So $\qquad\qquad\qquad x = 5$

Example 5.3 ▷ Solve the equation $x - 3 = 5$.

From what do you take 3 and end up with 5?

You know that $8 + 3 = 5$

So $\qquad x = 8$

1 Write each of these expressions using algebraic shorthand.

a	$3 \times n$	**b**	$5 \times n$	**c**	$7 \times m$	**d**	$8 \times t$
e	$a \times b$	**f**	$m \times n$	**g**	$p \times 5$	**h**	$q \times 4$
i	$m \div 3$	**j**	$5 \div n$	**k**	$7 \times w$	**l**	$k \times d$
m	$t \times 3$	**n**	$8 \div k$	**p**	$9 \times m$	**q**	$g \times h$

2 Copy and complete each of these.

a $6 + 2 = 2 + \boxed{}$ **b** $3 + 7 = 7 + \boxed{}$ **c** $m + n = n + \boxed{}$

d $3 + 4 = \boxed{} + 3$ **e** $5 + 8 = \boxed{} + 5$ **f** $k + h = \boxed{} + k$

g $5 + \boxed{} = 7 + 5$ **h** $6 + \boxed{} = 4 + 6$ **i** $x + \boxed{} = y + x$

j $\boxed{} + 9 = 9 + 1$ **k** $\boxed{} + 2 = 2 + 7$ **l** $\boxed{} + t = t + w$

m Explain what the answers above show you about addition.

3 Copy and complete each of these.

a $3 \times 2 = \boxed{} \times 3$ **b** $4 \times 5 = \boxed{} \times 4$ **c** $m \times n = \boxed{} \times m$

d $6 \times 5 = 5 \times \boxed{}$ **e** $7 \times 8 = 8 \times \boxed{}$ **f** $k \times h = h \times \boxed{}$

g $\boxed{} \times 9 = 9 \times 7$ **h** $\boxed{} \times 4 = 4 \times 6$ **i** $\boxed{} \times y = y \times x$

j $4 \times \boxed{} = 6 \times 4$ **k** $2 \times \boxed{} = 8 \times 2$ **l** $t \times \boxed{} = w \times t$

m Explain what the answers above show you about multiplication.

4 Calculate each of the following. (Remember, for example, that $3 - 7 = -4$.)

a $5 - 2 = \boxed{}$ **b** $9 - 4 = \boxed{}$ **c** $10 - 2 = \boxed{}$

    $2 - 5 = \boxed{}$ $4 - 9 = \boxed{}$ $2 - 10 = \boxed{}$

d Write down values for m and t which make

$\qquad m - t = t - m$

$\qquad \boxed{} - \boxed{} = \boxed{} - \boxed{}$

e Write down *two* more sets of values for m and t which make

$\qquad m - t = t - m$

$\qquad \boxed{} - \boxed{} = \boxed{} - \boxed{}$

$\qquad \boxed{} - \boxed{} = \boxed{} - \boxed{}$

f What must be special about m and t for $m - t$ to equal $t - m$?

5 Copy and complete each of these.

a $mp = m \times \boxed{}$ **b** $tv = \boxed{} \times v$ **c** $qr = \boxed{} \times \boxed{}$

d $\boxed{} = k \times g$ **e** $ab = \boxed{} \times b$ **f** $hp = h \times \boxed{}$

g $\boxed{} = t \times f$ **h** $pt = \boxed{} \times \boxed{}$

6 Solve each of the following equations, making correct use of the equals sign.

a $x + 1 = 11$ **b** $x - 3 = 5$ **c** $x + 4 = 19$ **d** $x - 1 = 13$

e $x + 3 = 9$ **f** $x - 3 = 12$ **g** $x + 7 = 12$ **h** $x - 5 = 10$

i $x - 12 = 33$ **j** $x + 3 = 80$ **k** $x + 8 = 73$ **l** $x - 7 = 65$

7 In each box, find the pairs of expressions that are equal to each other and write them down. For example:

$$\begin{array}{|c|} \hline 2 + 3 \\ 3 + 2 \\ 2 \times 3 \\ \hline \end{array} \quad 2 + 3 = 3 + 2$$

a
$$\begin{array}{|c|} \hline 2 \times 7 \\ 7 + 2 \\ 7 \times 2 \\ \hline \end{array}$$

b
$$\begin{array}{|c|} \hline m \times n \\ m + n \\ mn \\ \hline \end{array}$$

c
$$\begin{array}{|c|} \hline p \times q \\ q + p \\ pq \\ \hline \end{array}$$

d
$$\begin{array}{|c|} \hline 4 \div 2 \\ 2 \div 4 \\ \frac{2}{4} \\ \hline \end{array}$$

e
$$\begin{array}{|c|} \hline a - b \\ a \div b \\ \frac{a}{b} \\ \hline \end{array}$$

f
$$\begin{array}{|c|} \hline 4 \times 19 \\ 19 + 4 \\ 19 \times 4 \\ \hline \end{array}$$

g
$$\begin{array}{|c|} \hline 6 + x \\ 6x \\ x + 6 \\ \hline \end{array}$$

h
$$\begin{array}{|c|} \hline 3y \\ 3 + y \\ 3 \times y \\ \hline \end{array}$$

Extension Work

Only some of these statements are true. Write in a list those which are true.

1 $b + c = d + e$ is the same as $d + e = b + c$

2 $a - b = 6$ is the same as $6 = a - b$

3 $5x = x + 3$ is the same as $x = 5x + 3$

4 $5 - 2x = 8$ is the same as $8 = 2x - 5$

5 $ab - ba = T$ is the same as $T = ba - ab$

Two rules of algebra

Addition of terms

As you know, when you have, for example, $5 + 5 + 5$, you can write it simply as 3×5. Likewise in algebra, terms which use the same letter can be added together in the same way. For example:

$$m + m + m + m = 4 \times m = 4m$$

$$p + p + p = 3 \times p = 3p$$

Example 5.4 ▷ Simplify each of these.

a $d + d + d + d + d$ **b** $pq + pq + pq + pq + pq + pq$

a There are five ds, which simplify to $5 \times d = 5d$.

b There are six pqs, which simplify to $6 \times pq = 6pq$.

Raising a term to a power

A **power** or **index** tells you how many times to multiply a number or a term by itself. For example, 4^3 is a short way of writing $4 \times 4 \times 4$ to give the answer 64.

A term or number raised to a power is said to be in its **index form**.

Example 5.5 ▷ Write $m \times m \times m \times m$ in index form.

In index form m multiplied by itself four times is written as m^4.

That is, m to the power of four.

Example 5.6 ▷ Write, as simply as possible, $m \times m \times m \times m \times m$.

There are five of the ms multiplied together.

The simplest way of writing this is m^5.

Exercise 5B

1 Simplify each of the following expressions.

a $m + m$ **b** $k + k + k$ **c** $a + a + a + a$ **d** $d + d + d$
e $q + q + q + q$ **f** $t + t$ **g** $n + n + n + n$ **h** $g + g + g$
i $p + p + p$ **j** $w + w + w + w$ **k** $i + i + i + i + i$ **l** $a + a + a + a$

2 Copy and complete each of the following. For example:

$t + t + t + t = 4 \times t = 4t$

a $p + p + p = 3 \times p = \boxed{}$ **b** $m + m + m + m = 4 \times m = \boxed{}$

c $k + k + k = \boxed{} = \boxed{}$ **d** $h + h + h + h + h = \boxed{} = \boxed{}$

e $\boxed{} = 6 \times m = 6m$ **f** $\boxed{} = 5 \times p = \boxed{}$

g $\boxed{} = 3 \times g = \boxed{}$ **h** $\boxed{} = \boxed{} = 7n$

i $\boxed{} = \boxed{} = 5y$

3 Write each of the following expressions in index form.

a $n \times n \times n$ **b** $m \times m$ **c** $p \times p \times p \times p$ **d** $w \times w \times w$
e $m + m + m$ **f** $t + t + t + t$ **g** $k \times k \times k \times k$ **h** $y \times y \times y$
i $v \times v \times v \times v$ **j** $d + d + d + d + d$ **k** $t \times t \times t \times t \times t$ **l** $m \times m \times m$

4 Calculate each of the following powers.

a 3^3 **b** 4^2 **c** 2^4 **d** 4^3
e 5^3 **f** 2^3 **g** 3^4 **h** 10^2
i 10^3 **j** 2^5

5 Write each of the following as simply as possible.

a $n \times n$	**b** $m + m$	**c** $p \times p \times p$	**d** $w + w + w$
e $q \times q \times q \times q$	**f** $r + r + r + r$	**g** $k + k$	**h** $f \times f \times f$
i $v + v + v + v$	**j** $d \times d \times d \times d \times d$	**k** $q + q + q$	**l** $t \times t \times t \times t$

6 Copy and write out in full each of these.

a $3t = \dots\dots$ $\quad$ $t^3 = \dots\dots$ $\qquad$ **b** $4m = \dots\dots$ $\quad$ $m^4 = \dots\dots$

c $2k = \dots\dots$ $\quad$ $k^2 = \dots\dots$ $\qquad$ **d** $5w = \dots\dots$ $\quad$ $w^5 = \dots\dots$

e $3d = \dots\dots$ $\quad$ $d^3 = \dots\dots$

Extension Work

1 Show that two consecutive integers multiplied together always give an even number. (**Hint**: start with the first number as n.)

2 Show that any three consecutive integers multiplied together always give an even number.

Like terms and simplication

Like terms are those terms which are multiples of the same letter, or of the same combination of letters, or of powers of the same letter or combination of letters.
For example, a, $3a$, $\frac{1}{4}a$ and $-5a$ are all like terms. So are $2xy$, $7xy$ and $-8xy$ and x^2, $6x^2$ and $-3x^2$.

The multiples are called **coefficients**. So, in the above examples, 3, $\frac{1}{4}$, -5, 2, 7, -8, 6 and -3 are coefficients.

Only like terms can be added or subtracted to simplify an expression. For example:

$2xy + 7xy - 8xy$ simplifies to xy
$x^2 + 6x^2 - 3x^2$ simplifies to $4x^2$

Unlike terms cannot be combined.

Simplifying an expression means making it shorter by combining its terms where possible. This involves two steps:

● Collect like terms into groups.
● Combine the like terms in each group.

Example 5.7 ▷ Simplify $8p + 2q + 3p + 7s + 4q + 9$.

Write out the expression: $8p + 2q + 3p + 7s + 4q + 9$

Then collect like terms: $8p + 3p + 2q + 4q + 7s + 9$

Next, combine them: $11p + 6q + 7s + 9$

So, the expression in its simplest form is:

$11p + 6q + 7s + 9$

Example 5.8 ▷ Simplify $7x^2 + y^2 + 2x^2 - 3y^2 + 3z - 5$

Write out the expression: $7x^2 + y^2 + 2x^2 - 3y^2 + 3z - 5$

Then collect like terms: $7x^2 + 2x^2 + y^2 - 3y^2 + 3z - 5$

Next, combine them: $9x^2 \quad - \quad 2y^2 \quad + \quad 3z - 5$

So, the expression in its simplest form is:

$9x^2 - 2y^2 + 3z - 5$

Exercise 5C

1 Simplify each of these.

a	$2b + 3b$	**b**	$5x + 2x$	**c**	$6m + m$	**d**	$3m + m + 2m$
e	$7d - 3d$	**f**	$8g - 3g$	**g**	$4k - k$	**h**	$3t + 2t - t$

2

a	$5g + g - 2g$	**b**	$3x + 5x - 6x$	**c**	$4h + 3h - 5h$	**d**	$4q + 7q - 3q$
e	$5h - 2h + 4h$	**f**	$6x - 4x + 3x$	**g**	$3y - y + 4y$	**h**	$5d - 4d + 6d$
i	$8x - 2x - 3x$	**j**	$5m - m - 2m$	**k**	$8k - 3k - 2k$	**l**	$6n - 3n - n$

3 From each cloud, group together the like terms. For example:

> a 3b 2a
> 4b 5a b $\longrightarrow$ a, 2a, 3a
> b, 3b, 4b

a
> 3t g 5t
> 8g 9t 7g

b
> m 7p 4m
> 9p 10m
> 3p

c
> 4k 3m
> 5w 8m
> 7w 7m k

d
> x^2 t $5x^2$
> 3t $3x^2$ 4t

e
> y^2 2y 8y
> $7y^2$ $4y^2$
> 3y

f
> 7w 7g 3h
> 3g 9h 4w
> 3w 10g

4 Simplify each of these expressions.

a	$3b + 5 + 2b$	**b**	$2x + 7 + 3x$	**c**	$m + 2 + 5m$	**d**	$4k + 3k + 8$
e	$3x + 7 - x$	**f**	$5k + 4 - 2k$	**g**	$6p + 3 - 2p$	**h**	$5d + 1 - 4d$
i	$5m - 3 - 2m$	**j**	$6t - 4 - 2t$	**k**	$4w - 8 - 3w$	**l**	$5g - 1 - g$
m	$t + k + 4t$	**n**	$3x + 2y + 4x$	**p**	$2k + 3g + 5k$	**q**	$3h + 2w + w$
r	$5t - 2p - 3t$	**s**	$6n - 2t - 5n$	**t**	$p + 4q - 2q$	**u**	$3n + 2p - 3n$

5 Simplify each of these expressions.

a	$2t + 3g + 5t + 2g$	**b**	$4x + y + 2x + 3y$	**c**	$2m + k + 3m + 2k$
d	$5x + 3y - 2x + y$	**e**	$6m + 2p - 4m + 3p$	**f**	$3n + 4t - n + 3t$
g	$6k + 3g - 2k - g$	**h**	$7d + 4b - 5d - 3b$	**i**	$4q + 3p - 3q - p$
j	$4g - k + 2g - 3k$	**k**	$2x - 3y + 5x - 2y$	**l**	$4d - 3e - 3d - 2e$

6 Simplify each of these expressions.

  a $5x^2 + x^2$ **b** $6k^2 + 2k^2$ **c** $4m^2 + 3m^2$ **d** $6d^2 - 2d^2$

  e $5g^2 - 3g^2$ **f** $7a^2 - 5a^2$ **g** $5f^2 + 2f^2$ **h** $3y^2 - y^2$

  i $t^2 + 3t^2$ **j** $5h^2 - 2h^2$ **k** $6k^2 + k^2$ **l** $7m^2 - 3m^2$

7 Simplify each of these expressions.

  a $8x + 3 + 2x + 5$ **b** $5p + 2k + p + 3k$ **c** $9t + 3m + 2t + m$

  d $7k + 3t + 2t - 3k$ **e** $5m + 4p + p - 3m$ **f** $8w + 2d + 3d - 2w$

  g $6x + 2y + 4y + 2x$ **h** $8p + 3q + 4q - 3p$ **i** $3m + 2t + 3t - m$

1 Show that an odd number multiplied by another odd number always gives an odd number.

2 Show that an even number multiplied by another even number always gives an even number.

Using algebra with shapes

Example 5.9 Find **a** the perimeter and **b** the area of this rectangle.

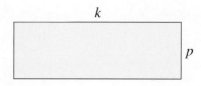

  a Perimeter $= 2(k + p) = 2k + 2p$

  b Area $= k \times p = kp$

Example 5.10 State the area of the shape as simply as possible:

First, split the shape into two parts A and B, as shown.

Shape A has the area $8x$ cm^2.

Shape B has the area $2y$ cm^2.

Total area is $(8x + 2y)$ cm^2.

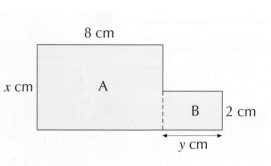

1 Write down, as simply as possible, the perimeter of each of these shapes:

a
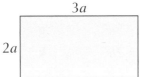
3a
2a

b
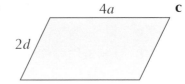
4a
2d

c
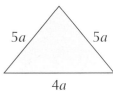
5a   5a
4a

d
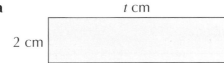
4x
2y   2y
2x

e
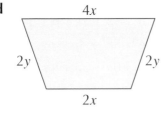
2p
3t   2p
3t   3t
2p

f
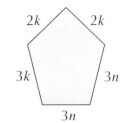
2k   2k
3k   3n
3n

2 What is the area of each rectangle.

a
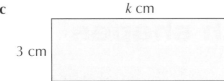
t cm
2 cm

b
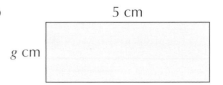
5 cm
g cm

c
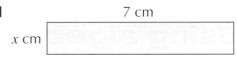
k cm
3 cm

d
7 cm
x cm

3 Write down, as simply as possible, the perimeter of each of these shapes.

a
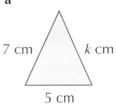
7 cm   k cm
5 cm

b
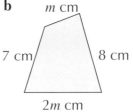
m cm
7 cm   8 cm
2m cm

c
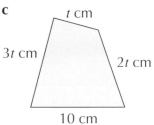
t cm
3t cm   2t cm
10 cm

4 Write down, as simply as possible, the area of each of these shapes.

a
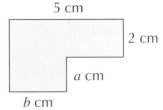
5 cm
2 cm
a cm
b cm

b
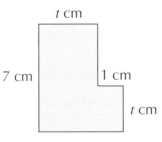
t cm
7 cm   1 cm
t cm

c
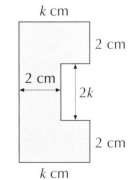
k cm
2 cm
2 cm   2k
2 cm
k cm

5 The expression in each box is made by adding the expressions in the two boxes it stands on. Copy the diagrams and fill in the missing expressions:

a

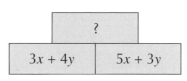

b

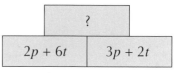

c

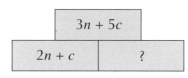

d

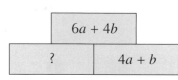

1 Use a spreadsheet to verify that $3a + 3b$ is always the same as $3(a + b)$

	A	B	C	D
1				

Put any number in A | Put any number in B | Put in the formula $3*A1 + 3*B1$ | Put in the formula $3*(A1 + B1)$

Copy the formula from C1 and D1 down to about C20 and D20. Check that for any type of number, negative and decimal, cell C = cell D for each row.

2 Use a spreadsheet to verify that $5a - 5b$ is always the same as $5 \times (a - b)$.

Expanding brackets

A number or a letter next to a bracket means that everything in the bracket must be multiplied by that number or letter if you want to remove the bracket.

This process is called **expanding** or **multiplying** out a bracket.

Example 5.11 ▷ Expand $4(2m + 3)$.

Multiply each term by 4: $4 \times 2m + 4 \times 3$
This gives: $8m + 12$

Example 5.12 ▷ Expand $3(5t - 2w - 3)$.

Multiply each term by 3: $3 \times 5t - 3 \times 2w - 3 \times 3$
This gives: $15t - 6w - 9$

Example 5.13 ▷ Expand and simplify $7x - 2(4y - x) - y$.

First, multiply each term in the bracket by -2: $7x - 8y + 2x - y$
Then collect like terms: $7x + 2x - 8y - y$
Finally, combine them: $9x - 9y$
So, the expression in its simplest form is: $9x - 9y$

Exercise 5E

1 Calculate each of the following by **i** expanding the bracket and **ii** using BODMAS, as the example shows:

i $2(5 + 3) = 2 \times 5 + 2 \times 3 = 10 + 6 = 16$
ii $2(5 + 3) = 2 \times 8 = 16$

a $3(4 + 2)$ **b** $5(3 + 1)$ **c** $4(2 + 3)$
d $6(3 + 4)$ **e** $8(5 - 2)$ **f** $10(5 - 2)$

2 Multiply out each of the following expressions.

a $2(x + 3)$ **b** $4(2m + 1)$ **c** $3(3k + 5)$ **d** $2(5n + 2)$
e $4(5 + 3t)$ **f** $3(2 + 5g)$ **g** $6(1 + 3h)$ **h** $5(3 + 2d)$
i $3(3a - 1)$ **j** $2(2 - 5c)$ **k** $8(1 - 2f)$ **l** $3(4 - 3b)$
m $2(3d + 2a)$ **n** $5(4e + 2)$ **p** $2(3x + 2y)$ **q** $7(2q + 5p)$
r $2(3q - 4p)$ **s** $3(5t - 3s)$ **t** $4(7w - 3k)$ **u** $5(4n - 3d)$

3 Expand and simplify each of the following expressions.

a $10m + 2(3m + 4)$ **b** $8t + 3(4t + 2)$ **c** $5k + 4(2k + 7)$
d $9g + 3(5 + 2g)$ **e** $7q + 4(3 + q)$ **f** $9h + 2(4 + 3h)$
g $8f + 2(4 + 3f)$ **h** $9k + 2(5 + k)$ **i** $10t + 3(1 + 5t)$

4 Expand and simplify each of the following expressions.

a $5(2h + 3) - 4h$ **b** $3(4t + 2p) - 5t$ **c** $4(3k + m) - 2m$
d $9g + 2(3g - 4)$ **e** $10t + 3(4g - t)$ **f** $7m + 2(5m - 4g)$
g $8m + 3(5m - k)$ **h** $12p + 2(3p - 4m)$ **i** $9h + 4(3h - 2p)$

5 Expand and simplify each of the following expressions.

a $2(2x + 3y) + 3(4x + 2y)$ **b** $3(3p + 2m) + 2(2p + 5m)$
c $4(5k + 4g) + 2(2k + 3g)$ **d** $3(3e + 2d) + 2(2d + 5e)$
e $5(5n + 2p) + 3(3n - 4p)$ **f** $4(5t + 3f) + 3(3t - 2f)$
g $3(p + 6d) + 5(2p - 3d)$ **h** $3(5x - 3y) + 2(4y - x)$

a Show, by taking a few examples, that the sum of any three consecutive integers is a multiple of 3.

b Do you think that the sum of any three consecutive integers is *always* a multiple of 3? Explain why.

c Show that the sum of four consecutive integers is never a multiple of 4.

d Is the sum of the five consecutive integers always a multiple of 5? Explain why.

What you need to know for level 4

○ Be able to recognise patterns in arithmetic to help to make calculations

What you need to know for level 5

○ Be able to recognise like terms, and to manipulate them

○ How to simplify expressions and expand brackets

National Curriculum SATs questions

LEVEL 4

1 *2000 Paper 1*

Here is the 65 times table.

a Use the 65 times table to help you to fill in the missing numbers.

$12 \times 65 = \ldots$

$20 \times 65 = \ldots$

b Use the 65 times table to help you to work out 16×65. Show how you do it.

$16 \times 65 = \ldots$

$1 \times 65 = 65$
$2 \times 65 = 130$
$3 \times 65 = 195$
$4 \times 65 = 260$
$5 \times 65 = 325$
$6 \times 65 = 390$
$7 \times 65 = 455$
$8 \times 65 = 520$
$9 \times 65 = 585$
$10 \times 65 = 650$

LEVEL 5

2 *2000 Paper 1*

Write each expression in its simplest form:

a $7 + 2t + 3t$

b $b + 7 + 2b + 10$

c $(3d + 5) + (d - 2)$

d $3m - (-m)$

3 *2002 Paper 1*

A teacher has a large pile of cards.

An expression for the total number of cards is $6n + 8$.

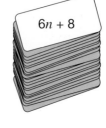

a The teacher puts the cards in two piles.

The number of cards in the first pile is $2n + 3$.

First pile   second pile

Write an expression to show the number of cards in the second pile.

b The teacher puts all the cards together.

Then he uses them to make two equal piles.

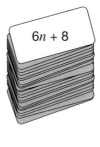

Write an expression to show the number of cards in one of the piles.

c The teacher puts all the cards together again, then he uses them to make two piles.

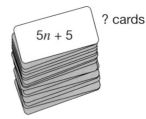

23 cards   ? cards

First pile   Second pile

There are 23 cards in the first pile.

How many cards are in the second pile?

Show your working.

CHAPTER 6

Shape, Space and Measures **2**

This chapter is going to show you	**What you should already know**
o how to find the perimeter and area of a rectangle o how to find the perimeter and area of a compound shape o how to read scales o how to find the surface area of a cuboid o how to convert from one metric unit to another	o How to find the perimeter of a shape o How to find the area of a shape by counting squares o The metric units for length, capacity and mass

Perimeter and area of rectangles

length (*l*)

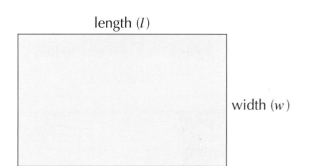

width (*w*)

The perimeter of a rectangle is the total distance around the shape.

Perimeter = 2 lengths + 2 widths

This can be written as a formula:

$P = 2l + 2w$

The units used to measure perimeter are mm, cm or m.

The area of the rectangle is the amount of space inside the shape.

Area = length × width

This can be written as a formula:

$A = l \times w$ or $A = lw$

The units used to measure area are mm², cm² or m².

Example 6.1

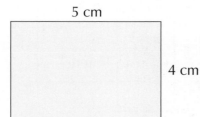

5 cm

4 cm

Find the perimeter and area of the rectangle.

$P = 2l + 2w = 2 \times 5 + 2 \times 4 = 10 + 8 = 18$ cm

$A = lw = 5 \times 4 = 20$ cm²

1 Find **i** the perimeter and **ii** the area of the each of the following rectangles by measuring the length of the sides of each one.

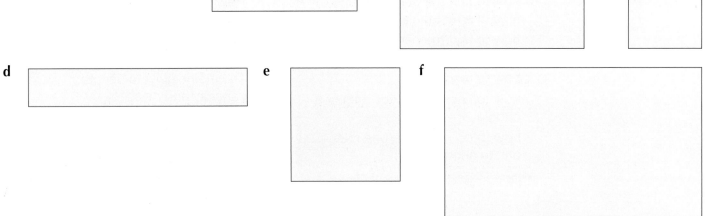

a

b

c

d

e

f

2 Find **i** the perimeter and **ii** the area of the each of the following rectangles. Remember to use the correct units.

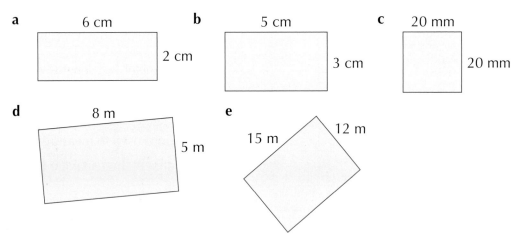

a 6 cm, 2 cm

b 5 cm, 3 cm

c 20 mm, 20 mm

d 8 m, 5 m

e 15 m, 12 m

3 Find the area of each of the following rectangles. Remember to use the correct units.

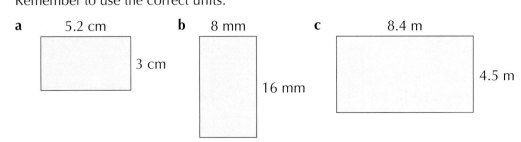

a 5.2 cm, 3 cm

b 8 mm, 16 mm

c 8.4 m, 4.5 m

4 A bungalow has two bedrooms.

The first bedroom measures 4.6 m by 3.8 m and the second bedroom is 4.1 m square. Which bedroom has the greater perimeter?

5 A room is 6 m long and 3.8 m wide. A carpet measuring 4.2 m by 3 m is placed on the floor of the room. Find the area of the floor not covered by carpet.

Estimate the area of each of the irregular shapes drawn on the centimetre square grid below.

To do this, mark with a dot each square that is at least half-covered by the shape, and then count how many squares contain a dot.

For example: dots have been marked on each square that is at least half-covered by shape 1. There are 15 dots in total, so the estimate of the area of shape 1 is 15 cm².

You may wish to start by tracing the shapes on to centimetre-squared paper.

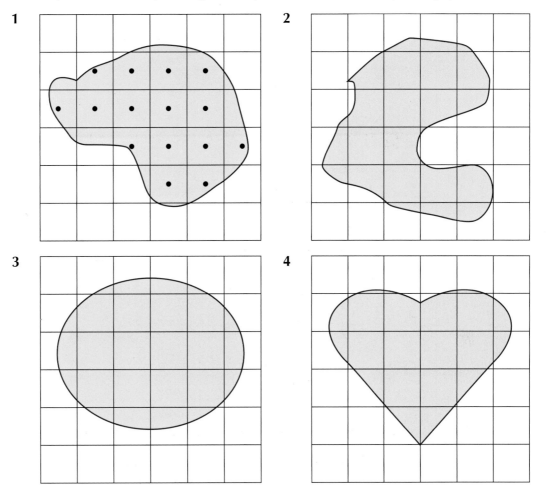

Perimeter and area of compound shapes

A compound shape is a shape that is made by combining other simple shapes, such as squares, rectangles and triangles.

The example shows you how to find the perimeter and area of a compound shape made from two rectangles.

Example 6.2 Find the perimeter and area of the
following compound shape.

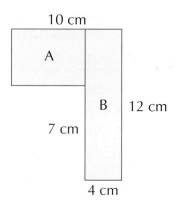

First copy the shape, then find and
label the lengths of any sides which
aren't already shown.

Now the perimeter and area of the
compound shape can be worked
out as follows:

$P = 10 + 12 + 4 + 7 + 6 + 5$
    $= 44$ cm

Total area = Area of A + Area of B
            $= 6 \times 5 + 12 \times 4$
            $= 30 + 48$
            $= 78$ cm^2

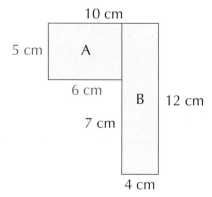

Exercise 6B

1 Find **i** the perimeter and **ii** the area of each of the following compound shapes. Start
by copying the diagrams and splitting them up into rectangles.

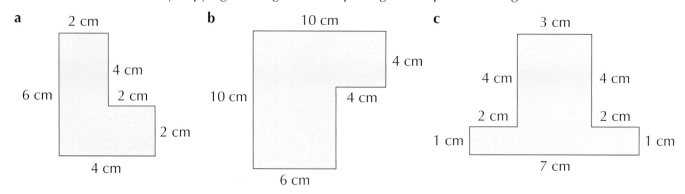

2 Find **i** the perimeter and **ii** the area of each of the following compound shapes.

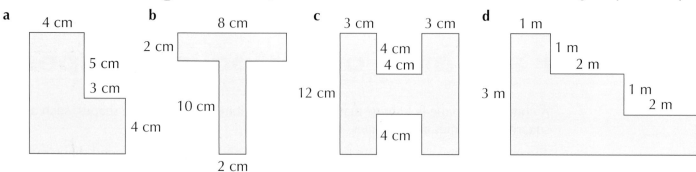

3 Sandra makes a picture frame from a rectangular piece of card for a photograph of her favourite group.

    a   Find the area of the photograph.

    b   Find the area of the card she uses.

    c   Find the area of the border.

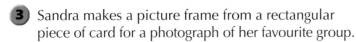

20 cm   14 cm   24 cm   30 cm

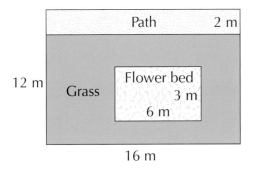

Path   2 m
12 m   Grass   Flower bed   3 m   6 m
16 m

4 A garden is in the shape of a rectangle measuring 16 m by 12 m.

Calculate the area of the grass in the garden.

5 How many rectangles can you draw with a fixed perimeter of 20 cm but each one having a different area? You may use centimetre-squared paper to draw any diagrams.

Extension Work

The diagram on the right is a bathroom floor.

It is going to be covered with square tiles. Each tile measures 20 cm by 20 cm. Tiles can be cut in half.

How many tiles are needed to cover the floor?

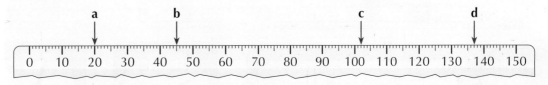

250 cm

60 cm

160 cm

150 cm

Reading scales

It is important in subjects such as Science and Technology to be able to read scales accurately.

When reading a scale always make sure that you first work out the size of each division on the scale.

Example 6.3   What length is each arrow pointing to on the ruler shown below?

a   b   c   d

0   10   20   30   40   50   60   70   80   90   100   110   120   130   140   150

Each small division on the ruler is 1 mm or 0.1 cm.

So, the arrows are pointing to the following lengths:

a   2 cm   **b**   4.5 cm   **c**   10.2 cm   **d**   13.7 cm

1 Write down the number that each arrow is pointing to on each of the number lines below.

a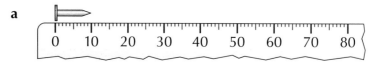

b

c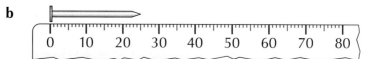

d

2 Write down the length of each of the following nails. Give your answer
   i in centimetres   **ii** in millimetres.

a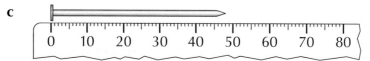

b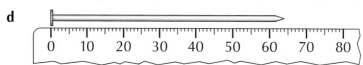

c

d

3 Write down the mass shown on each of the following scales.

a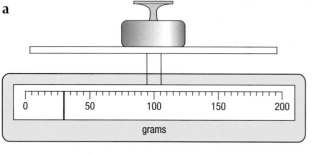

b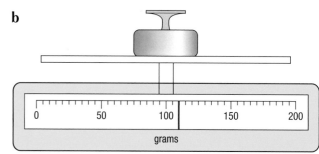

c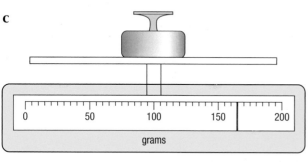

d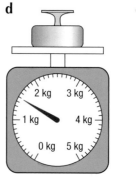

e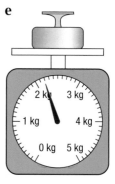

f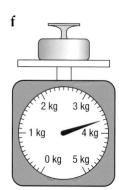

4 Write down the volume of water in each of the following jugs.

a    **b**    **c**   **d**

5 Each thermometer below shows the temperature in °C.

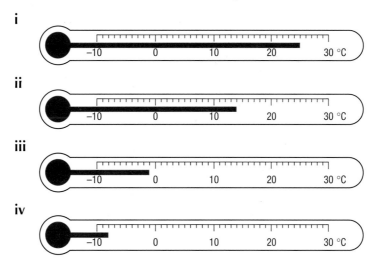

i

ii

iii

iv

  a Write down the temperatures marked i, ii, iii and iv.
  b What temperature is 5 degrees higher than 2°C?
  c What temperature is 5 degrees higher than –2°C?
  d What temperature is 5 degrees lower than –2°C?
  e The temperature changes from 10°C to –5°C.
     By how many degrees has the temperature changed?

Extension Work

1 A box contains the following:
  four 10 g weights
  four 20 g weights
  four 50 g weights
  four 100 g weights

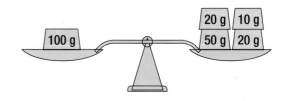

  One combination of weights that will balance the scales is shown.

  How many other ways to balance the scales can you find?

2 For this activity you will need some weighing scales.

  Weigh some objects in the classroom, giving your answer as accurately as possible.

Surface area of cubes and cuboids

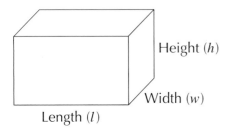

Height (*h*)

Width (*w*)

Length (*l*)

The surface area of a cuboid is found by calculating the total area of its six faces.

> Area of top face = length × width = *lw*
>
> Area of bottom face = *lw*
>
> Area of front face = length × height = *lh*
>
> Area of back face = *lh*
>
> Area of right end face = width × height = *wh*
>
> Area of left end face = *wh*

So, the surface area of the cuboid is:

$S = lw + lw + lh + lh + wh + wh$

$S = 2lw + 2lh + 2wh$

Example 6.4 ▷ Find the surface area of this cuboid.

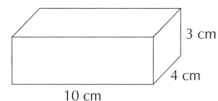

3 cm

4 cm

10 cm

$$S = (2 \times 10 \times 4) + (2 \times 10 \times 3) + (2 \times 4 \times 3)$$
$$= 80 + 60 + 24$$
$$= 164 \text{ cm}^2$$

Exercise 6D

1 Find the surface area for each of the following cuboids.

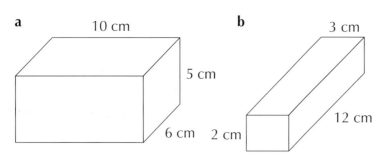 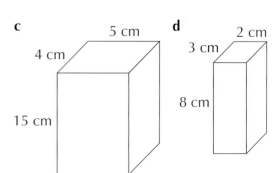

a 10 cm, 5 cm, 6 cm

b 3 cm, 2 cm, 12 cm

c 5 cm, 4 cm, 15 cm

d 2 cm, 3 cm, 8 cm

2 Find the surface area of this unit cube.

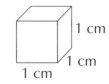

1 cm

1 cm

1 cm

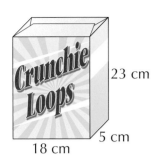

23 cm

5 cm

18 cm

3 Find the surface area for each of the cubes with the following edge lengths.

    a   2 cm   **b**   5 cm   **c**   10 cm   **d**   8 m

4 Find the surface area of the cereal packet on the left.

5 Find the surface area of the outside of this open water tank.
(A cuboid without a top.)

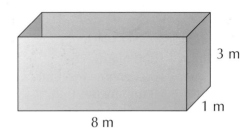

3 m

1 m

8 m

6 Find the total surface area of this 3-D shape. Start by drawing each face separately and finding the lengths of any unknown sides. Then work out the area of each face and add them together to get the total surface area.

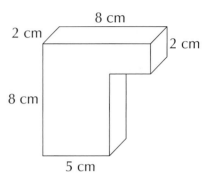

2 cm   8 cm   2 cm

8 cm

5 cm

7 Six unit (centimetre) cubes are placed together to make the following 3-D shapes.

a

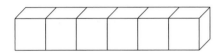

b

c

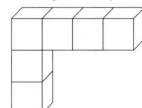

Find the surface area of each shape.

Extension Work

1 **Estimating**

Estimate the surface area for various everyday objects in the shape of cuboids.

Check your estimate by measuring.

20 cm

16 cm

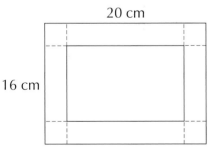

2 **Open box problem**

An open box is made from a piece of card, measuring 20 cm by 16 cm, by cutting off a square from each corner.

Investigate the surface area of the open box formed for different sizes of square cut off.

You may wish to put your data on a computer spreadsheet.

3 **Cubes to cuboids.**

Twenty unit cubes are arranged to form a cuboid.

How many different cuboids can you make?

Which one has the greatest surface area?

Converting one metric unit into another

Below are the common metric units which you need to know. Also given are the relationships between these units.

Length

Larger unit		*Smaller unit*
1 kilometre (km)	=	1000 metres (m)
1 metre (m)	=	100 centimetres (cm)
1 centimetre (cm)	=	10 millimetres (mm)

Capacity

Larger unit		*Smaller unit*
1 litre (l)	=	100 centilitres (l)
1 litre (l)	=	1000 millilitres (ml)

Mass

Larger unit		*Smaller unit*
1 kilogram (kg)	=	1000 grams (g)

To convert a smaller unit into a larger unit you need to *divide* by the amount given in the table above.

To convert a larger unit to a smaller unit you need to *multiply* by the amount given in the table above.

Example 6.5

a Change 7 cm to mm.

10 mm = 1 cm and you are changing a larger unit to a smaller unit, so you need to multiply by 10.

7 × 10 = 70, so 7 cm = 70 mm.

b Convert 2500 g to kg.

1000 g = 1 kg and you are changing a smaller unit to a larger unit, so you need to divide by 1000.

2500 ÷ 1000 = 2.5, so 2500 g = 2.5 kg

When you are adding or subtracting two metric quantities in different units, you must change them both to the same unit first. It is usually easier to change them both to the smaller unit.

Example 6.6

What is 800 m + 2 km?

2 km = 2000 m, so 800 m + 2 km = 800 m + 2000 m
= 2800 m

If you were asked for the answer in kilometres, you could then convert this as normal:

2800 ÷ 1000 = 2.8 km

Exercise 6E

1 Change each of the following lengths to centimetres:

    a 80 mm   **b** 120 mm   **c** 55 mm   **d** 136 mm   **e** 9 mm

2 Change each of the following lengths to centimetres:

    a 2 m   **b** 10 m   **c** 4.5 m   **d** 3.8 m   **e** 0.4 m

3 Change each of the following lengths to kilometres:

    a 3000 m   **b** 10000 m   **c** 3500 m   **d** 6700 m   **e** 800 m

4 Change each of the following capacities to centilitres:

    a 4 l   **b** 7 l   **c** 1.5 l   **d** 8.2 l   **e** 0.3 l

5 Change each of the following masses to grams

    a 5 kg   **b** 9 kg   **c** 2.5 kg   **d** 3.2 kg   **e** 0.2 kg

6 Work out each of the following; give your answer in the smaller unit:

    a 2 cm + 7 mm   **b** 3 km − 800 m   **c** 2.5 l + 70 cl   **d** 1.4 kg − 300 g

7 The two carpets below are joined together to make a longer carpet. How long will the carpet be? Give your answer in metres.

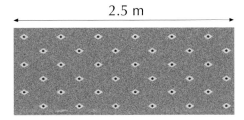
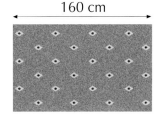

2.5 m   160 cm

8 Jenny carries home the shopping shown below. Find the total weight that she has to carry. Give your answer in kilograms.

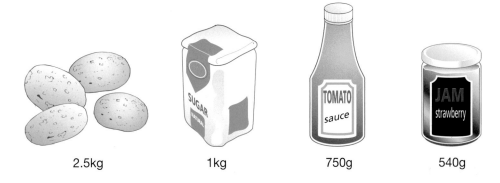

2.5kg   1kg   750g   540g

9 Simon pours four glasses of lemonade from a 2 l bottle. If each glass holds 200 cl, how much lemonade is left in the bottle? Give your answer in centilitres.

10 The distance round a school running track is 600 m. During a PE lesson, Hardeep completes 8 circuits. How far does he run altogether? Give your answer in kilometres.

Extension Work

How big is a million?

1 Change one million millimetres into kilometres.

2 Change one million grams into kilograms.

3 How long is one million seconds? Give your answer in days, hours, minutes and seconds.

National Curriculum SATs questions

LEVEL 4

1 *2002 Paper 1*

    a What is the area of this rectangle?

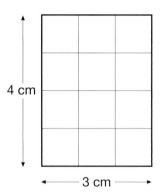

    b I use the rectangle to make four triangles.

    Each triangle is the same size.

    What is the area of **one** of the triangles?

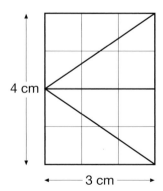

c I use the four triangles to make a trapezium.

What is the area of the trapezium?

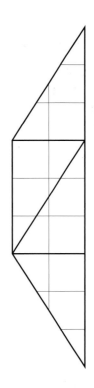

2 *1997 Paper 2*

a The scale shows how long Laura was
when she was born.

How long was Laura?

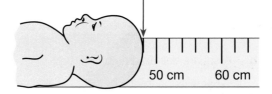

b When Laura was one month old she
was put on the scales.

What mass do the scales show?

c Now Laura is older.

She is 1.03m tall.

Write Laura's height in centimetres.

LEVEL 5

3 *2001 Paper 2*

a Which rectangles below have an area of 12cm²?

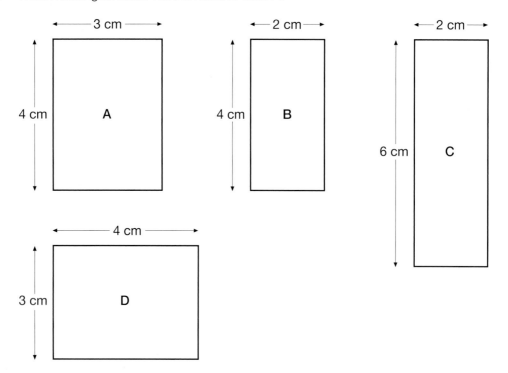

b A square has an area of 100 cm².

What is its perimeter?

Show your working.

4 *1999 Paper 1*

The diagram shows a rectangle 18cm long and 14cm wide.

It has been split into four smaller rectangles.

Write the area of each small rectangle on a copy of the diagram.

One has been done for you.

What is the area of the whole rectangle?

What is 18 × 14?

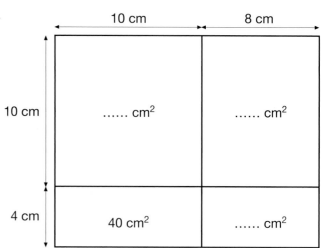

This chapter is going to show you

- how to draw mapping diagrams from functions
- how to identify a function from its inputs and outputs
- how to spot patterns in sets of coordinates
- how to draw distance–time graphs

What you should already know

- How to use a function
- How to plot coordinates

Linear functions

A linear function is a simple rule that involves any of the following:

Addition	Subtraction	Multiplication	Division

Mapping diagrams can illustrate these functions, as shown in Example 7.1.

Example 7.1 ▷ Draw a mapping diagram to illustrate:

First, draw two number lines. The top line is for the inputs and the bottom line shows the place to which each input maps with the function (see top of next page). Both number lines in this example are shown from 0 to 7.

So, for the function

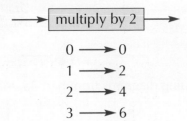

And so on.

Now draw arrows between the two number lines to show the place to which each number maps:

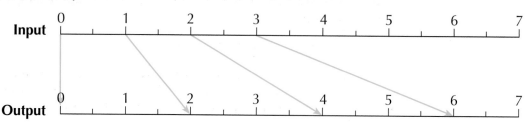

Of course, both number lines go on for ever, and each contains hundreds of numbers. But only a small part is needed to show the pattern of mapping.

1 a Copy the mapping diagram for the function ⟶ add 3 ⟶ .

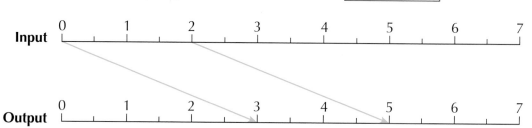

b On the diagram map the input values 3 and 4.

c Now map the following values:

    i   0.5   **ii**   1.5   **iii**   2.5   **iv**   3.5

2 a Using two number lines from 0 to 10, draw a mapping diagram to illustrate each of these functions (map each whole-number).

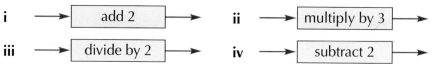

    i ⟶ add 2 ⟶   **ii** ⟶ multiply by 3 ⟶

    iii ⟶ divide by 2 ⟶   **iv** ⟶ subtract 2 ⟶

b In each of your mapping diagrams from part **2ai** and **ii**, draw the lines from the inputs 0.5, 1.5 and 2.5.

3 a Using two number lines from 0 to 15, draw a mapping diagram to illustrate each of these functions.

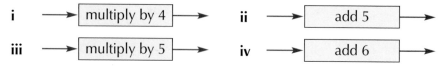

    i ⟶ multiply by 4 ⟶   **ii** ⟶ add 5 ⟶

    iii ⟶ multiply by 5 ⟶   **iv** ⟶ add 6 ⟶

b In each of your mapping diagrams from part **3a**, map the input values 0.5, 1.5 and 2.5.

a Using number lines from 0 to 10, draw a mapping diagram of the function

$$\longrightarrow \boxed{\text{multiply by 2}} \longrightarrow$$

b For each of the arrows drawn on your mapping diagram, extend the arrow line backwards towards the line that joins both zeros. All the arrow lines should meet at the same point on this line.

c Repeat the above for the function

$$\longrightarrow \boxed{\text{multiply by 3}} \longrightarrow$$

Do these arrows also join at a point on the line joining the zeros?

d Do you think all similar functions such as

$$\longrightarrow \boxed{\text{multiply by 4}} \longrightarrow$$

have this property?

Finding a function from its inputs and outputs

Any function will have a set of outputs for a particular set of inputs. When you can identify the outputs for particular inputs, then you can identify the function.

Example 7.2 State the function that maps the inputs {0, 1, 2, 3} to {0, 5, 10, 15}.

The input 0 maps to 0. Hence the function uses no addition.

Notice that each time the input increases by 1, the output increases by 4. This suggests that the function is: $\boxed{\text{multiply by 5}}$

A check that 1 does map to 5 and 2 to 10 shows that this function is the correct one.

Exercise 7B

1 State the function that maps the following inputs with their respective outputs:

    a {0, 1, 2, 3} $\longrightarrow$ {4, 5, 6, 7}

    b {0, 1, 2, 3} $\longrightarrow$ {0, 4, 8, 12}

    c {0, 1, 2, 3} $\longrightarrow$ {0, 7, 14, 21}

    d {0, 1, 2, 3} $\longrightarrow$ {7, 8, 9, 10}

    e {0, 1, 2, 3} $\longrightarrow$ {0, 10, 20, 30}

2 State the function that maps the following inputs with their respective outputs.

    a {0, 1, 3, 5} $\longrightarrow$ {9, 10, 12, 14}

    b {0, 3, 4, 5} $\longrightarrow$ {0, 9, 12, 15}

    c {1, 3, 4, 5} $\longrightarrow$ {9, 11, 12, 13}

    d {0, 1, 2, 3} $\longrightarrow$ {10, 11, 12, 13}

3 State which function maps the inputs {2, 4, 7, 8} to:

    a   {6, 12, 21, 24}   **b**   {7, 9, 12, 13}   **c**   {16, 32, 56, 64}

4 State which function maps the following inputs

    i   {0, 8, 16}   **ii**   {1, 2, 3}   **iii**   {10, 18, 26}

    to {8, 16, 24}.

5 What are the functions that generate the following mixed outputs from the given mixed inputs? [*Hint*: First put each set of numbers in sequence.]

    {2, 4, 1, 3} ⟶ {8, 10, 11, 9}

    {4, 2, 3, 5} ⟶ {20, 16, 8, 12}

    {6, 3, 5, 4} ⟶ {10, 9, 11, 8}

    {8, 10, 7, 9} ⟶ {7, 6, 8, 5}

    {3, 2, 1, 0} ⟶ {6, 0, 9, 3}

Extension Work

Look at these simple functions:

By using any two of them, you can create six different combined functions, such as:

{2, 3, 4, 5} ⟶ | multiply by 2 | ⟶ | add 3 | ⟶ {7, 9, 11, 13}

Draw a diagram like the one above for the other five possible combined functions.

Graphs from functions

There are different ways to write functions down. For example, the function:

⟶ | add 3 | ⟶

can also be written as:

$$y = x + 3$$

where the inputs are x and the outputs are y.

The second way of writing a function makes it easier to draw a graph of the function.

Every function produces a graph. This is drawn by working out from the function a set of **coordinates** for its graph. **Note** The graph of every linear function is a straight line.

Example 7.3 Draw a graph of the function

⟶ [multiply by 3] ⟶ or $y = 3x$

First, draw up a table of simple values for x.

x	0	1	2	3
$y = 3x$	0	3	6	9

So, the coordinate pairs are:

(0, 0)   (1, 3)   (2, 6)   (3, 9)

Next, plot each point on a grid, and join up all the points.

Note This straight line-line graph has hundreds of other coordinates, *all* of which obey the same rule of the function: that is, $y = 3x$. Choose any points on the line that have not been plotted and you will see that this is true.

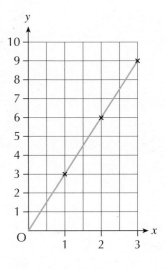

Exercise 7C

1 a Complete the table below for the function ⟶ [add 3] ⟶ or $y = x + 3$.

x	0	1	2	3
$y = x + 3$	3			

b Draw a grid with its x-axis from 0 to 3 and its y-axis from 0 to 7.

c Use the table to help you to draw, on the grid, the graph of the function $y = x + 3$.

2 a Complete the table below for the function ⟶ [multiply by 2] ⟶ or $y = 2x$.

x	0	1	2	3
$y = 2x$	0			

b Draw a grid with its x-axis from 0 to 3 and its y-axis from 0 to 7.

c Use the table to help you to draw, on the grid, the graph of the function $y = 2x$.

3 a Complete the table below for the function ⟶ [subtract 1] ⟶ or $y = x - 1$:

x	0	1	2	3	4
$y = x - 1$	−1				

b Draw a grid with its x-axis from 0 to 4 and its y-axis from −1 to 4.

c Use the table to help you to draw, on the grid, the graph of the function $y = x - 1$.

4 **a** Complete the table below for the function  ⟶ divide by 2 ⟶ or $y = \frac{1}{2}x$.

x	0	1	2	3	4
$y = \frac{1}{2}x$	0	0.5			

b Draw a grid with its x-axis from 0 to 4 and its y-axis from 0 to 4.

c Use the table to help you to draw, on the grid, the graph of the function $y = \frac{1}{2}x$.

5 **a** Complete the table below for the functions shown.

x	0	1	2	3	4
y = x + 5				8	
y = x + 3			5		
y = x + 1	1	2			
y = x − 1	−1	0			
y = x − 3	−3		−1		

b Draw a grid with its x-axis from 0 to 4 and its y-axis from −4 to 10.

c Draw the graph for each function in the table above.

d What two properties do you notice about each line?

e Use the properties you have noticed to draw the graph of each of these functions.

   i $y = x + 2.5$ **ii** $y = x - 1.5$

6 **a** Complete the table below for the functions shown.

x	0	1	2	3	4
y = x				3	
y = 2x			4		
y = 3x	0	3			
y = 4x					16
y = 5x			10		

b Draw a grid with its x-axis from 0 to 4 and y-axis from 0 to 20.

c Draw the graph for each function in the table above.

d What do you notice about each line?

e Use the properties you have noticed to draw the graph of each of these functions:

   i $y = 1.5x$ **ii** $y = 3.5x$

Rules with coordinates

Number puzzles and sequences can be made in coordinates as well as ordinary numbers.

Example 7.4

There is a dot in each of the rectangles in the diagram. The dots are in the corners that are defined by the coordinates (2, 1), (4, 1), (6, 1), (8, 1).

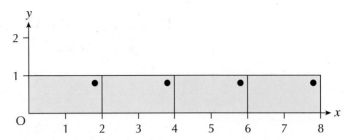

a If the pattern of rectangles continues, write down the coordinates of the next four corners with dots.

b Explain how you can tell that there will be no dot at the coordinate (35, 1).

Looking at the *x*-coordinates (the left-hand numbers), you will notice that the numbers go up in the sequence 2, 4, 6, 8 (even numbers). So, the next four will be 10, 12, 14 and 16.

Looking at the *y*-coordinates (the right-hand numbers), you will notice that the numbers are all 1.

a So, the next four coordinates will be (10, 1), (12, 1), (14, 1), (16, 1).

b Since 35 is not an even number, (35, 1) cannot be the coordinates of a corner with a dot.

Exercise 7D

1 Joy has 20 rectangular tiles like the one shown.

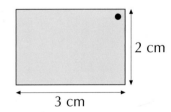

She places all these tiles in a row.
She starts her row like this:

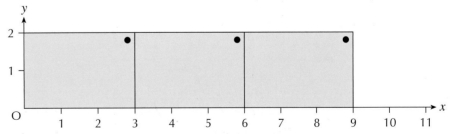

For each rectangular tile, Joy writes down the coordinates of the corner which has a dot. The coordinates of the first corner are (3, 2).

a Write down the coordinates of the next six corners which have a dot.

b Look at the numbers in the coordinates. Describe two things you notice.

c Joy thinks that (41, 2) are the coordinates of one of the corners with a dot. Explain why she is wrong.

d What are the coordinates of the dotted corner in the 20th tile?

2 Joy now places her tiles in a pattern like this:

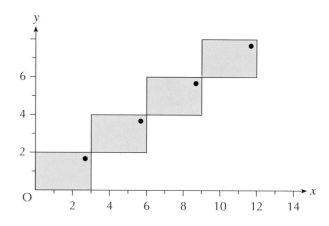

a Write down the coordinates of the first six corners which have a dot.

b Look at the numbers in the coordinates. Describe two things you notice.

c Joy thinks that that (24, 16) are the coordinates of one of the corners with a dot. Explain why she is right.

d What are the coordinates of the dotted corner in the 20th tile?

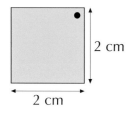

2 cm

2 cm

3 Alan has 20 square tiles like the one shown on the left.

He places all these tiles in a row. He starts his row like this:

For each square tile, Alan writes down the coordinates of the corner with a dot. The coordinates of the first corner are (2, 2).

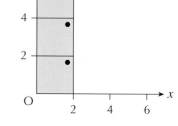

a Write down the coordinates of the next six corners which have a dot.

b Look at the numbers in the coordinates. Describe two things you notice.

c Alan thinks that (2, 22) are the coordinates of one of the corners with a dot. Explain why he is right.

d What are the coordinates of the dotted corner in the 20th tile?

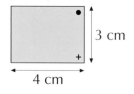

3 cm

4 cm

4 Ben has 20 rectangular tiles like the one shown on the left.

He places all these tiles in a pattern on the left. He starts his pattern like this:

For each rectangular tile, he writes down the coordinates of the corner which has a dot. The coordinates of the first corner are (4, 3).

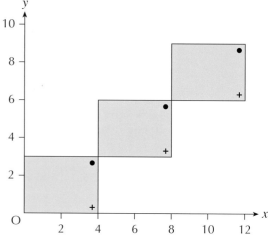

a Write down the coordinates of the next six corners which have a dot.

b Look at the numbers in the coordinates. Describe two things you notice.

c Ben thinks that (24, 10) are the coordinates of one of the corners which have a dot. Explain why he is wrong.

d What are the coordinates of the dotted corner in the 20th tile?

For each rectangular tile, Ben now writes down the coordinates of the corner which has a +. The coordinates of the first corner are (4, 0)

e Write down the coordinates of the next six corners which have a +.

f Look at the numbers in the coordinates. Describe two things you notice.

g Ben thinks that (28, 16) are the coordinates of one of the corners which have a +. Explain why he is wrong.

h What are the coordinates of the corner with a + in the 20th tile?

Distance—time graphs

A distance—time graph gives information about how someone or something has travelled.

Distance—time graphs are often used to describe journeys, as in Example 7.5.

Example 7.5

Mohammed set off from home at 8.00 AM to pick up a parcel from the post office. At 8.30 AM he arrived at the post office, having walked 4 km. He waited 15 minutes, got his parcel and then walked back home in 20 minutes.

Draw a distance time graph of Mohammed's journey. Estimate how far from home he was at:

a 8.10 AM   **b** 9.00 AM

The key coordinates (time and distance from home) are:
- Starting out (8.00 AM, 0 km).
- Arrival at the post office (8.30 AM, 4 km).
- Leaving the post office (8.45 AM, 4 km).
- Return home (9.05 AM, 0 km)

Using the information above, plot the points and draw the graph.

Note The axes are clearly and accurately labelled, with precisely placed divisions. It is important to do this when you are drawing graphs.

You can now use your graph to answer the questions.

a At 8.10 AM, Mohammed was 1.3 km from home.

b At 9.00 AM, Mohammed was 1 km from home.

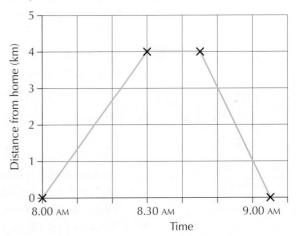

Exercise 7E

1 a Draw a grid with the following scales:
Horizontal axis: Time, from 10.00 AM to 11.30 AM, with 1 cm to 10 minutes.
Vertical axis: Distance from home, from 0 to 8 km, with 1 cm to 1 km.

b Draw on your grid the travel graph which shows the following journey.
Gemma left home at 10.00 AM, cycled 3 km to a friend's house, arriving there at 10.15 AM. She was not at home, so Gemma cycled another 4 km in the same direction to another friend's house, arriving there at 10.35 AM. Gemma's friend was in. Gemma stayed there for 15 minutes. Then she went back home, arriving at 11.30 AM.

c Approximately how far from home was Gemma at the following times?
i 10.20 AM   **ii** 11.15 AM

2 a Draw a grid with the following scales:

Horizontal axis: Time, from 8.00 AM to 10.30 AM, with 1 cm to 10 minutes.

Vertical axis: Distance, from 0 to 20 km. With 1 cm to 2 km.

b Draw on your grid the travel graph which shows the following journey.

Anne started her sponsored walk at 8.00 AM.

She walked the first 5 km in 20 minutes.

She walked the next 5 km in 30 minutes, then stopped to rest for ten minutes.

She walked the next 5 km in 25 minutes, then stopped for fifteen minutes.

She walked the last 5 km in 40 minutes.

c At about what time had she walked the following distances?

   i   3 km   **ii**   8 km   **iii**   17 km

3 a Draw a grid with the following scales:

Horizontal axis: Time, from 7.00 AM to 1.00 PM, with 2 cm to 1 hour.

Vertical axis: Distance from home, from 0 to 600 km, with 1 cm to 50 km.

b Draw on your grid the travel graph which shows the following journey.

A bus set off from Sheffield at 7.00 AM, travelling to Cornwall.

At 9.00 AM the bus had travelled 150 km. It then stopped for 30 minutes.

At 11.00 AM the bus had travelled a further 250 km. It again stopped for 30 minutes.

The bus arrived at its destination at 1.00 PM, after a journey of 600 km.

c Approximately how far from Sheffield was the bus at these times?

   i   8.00 AM   **ii**   10.30 AM   **iii**   12 noon

4 a Draw a grid with the following scales:

Horizontal axis: Time, from 2.00 PM to 5.00 PM, with 1 cm to 30 minutes.

Vertical axis, Distance from home, showing 0 to 60 km, with 1 cm to 10 km.

b Draw on your grid the travel graph which shows the following journey.

A seagull left its nest at 2.00 PM, flying out to sea.

After 30 minutes, the bird had flown 10 km. It then stopped on the top of a lighthouse for 30 minutes.

The bird then kept flying out to sea and at 4.00 PM landed on a boat mast, 25 km from its nest.

The wind picked up and the bird flew again out to sea, stopping at 5.00 PM, 60 km from its nest.

c How far was the bird from its nest at the following times?

   i   3.30 PM   **ii**   4.45 PM

Extension Work

At 10.00 AM, Joy set off from her home to walk towards Nicola's home, 500 metres away. At the same time, Nicola set off from her home to walk towards Joy's home.

Both girls were walking with their eyes down and didn't see each other as they passed. Joy arrived at Nicola's house at ten past ten. Nicola arrived at Joy's house at six minutes past ten.

a At what time did they pass each other?

b For how long were they within 100 metres of each other?

National Curriculum SATs questions

LEVEL 4

1 *1995 Paper 2*

Marc has ten square tiles like this:

Marc places all the square tiles in a row.
He starts his row like this:

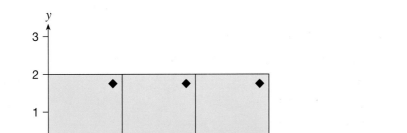

For each square tile, he writes down the coordinates of the corner which has a ◆.

The coordinates of the first corner are (2, 2).

a   Write down the coordinates of the next five corners which have a ◆.

b   Look at the numbers in the coordinates. Describe two things you notice.

c   Marc thinks that (17, 2) are the coordinates of one of the corners which have a ◆. Explain why he is wrong.

d   Sam has some bigger square tiles, like this:

She places them next to each other in a row, like Marc's tiles. Write down the coordinates of the first two corners which have a ●.

2 *1999 Paper 1*

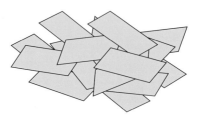

Daniel has some parallelogram tiles.

He puts them on a grid, in a continuing pattern. He numbers each tile.

The diagram shows part of the pattern of tiles on the grid.

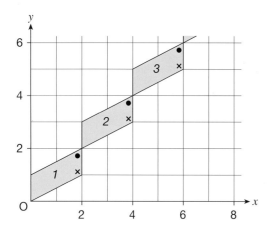

Daniel marks the top right hand corner of each tile with a ●. The coordinates of the corner with a ● on tile number 3 are (6, 6).

a What are the coordinates of the corner with a ● on tile number 4?

b What are the coordinates of the corner with a ● on tile number 20? Explain how you worked out your answer.

c Daniel says:

One tile in the pattern has a ● in the corner at (25, 25).

Explain why Daniel is wrong.

d Daniel marks the bottom right hand corner of each tile with a ✗. Copy and complete the table to show the coordinates of each corner with a ✗.

Tile number	Coordinates of the corner with a ✗
1	(..2.., ..1..)
2	(......, ...)
3	(......, ...)
4	(......, ...)

Copy and complete these statements.

e Tile number 7 has a ✗ in the corner at (......, ...).

f Tile number ...... has a ✗ in the corner at (20, 19).

LEVEL 5

3 *2000 Paper 2*

The graph shows my journey in a lift.

I got in the lift at floor number 10.

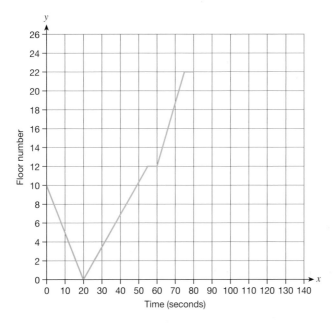

a The lift stopped at two different floors before I got to floor number 22.

b For how long was I in the lift while it was moving?

c After I got out of the lift at floor number 22, the lift went directly to the ground floor.

It took 45 seconds.

Which of the graphs below shows the rest of the lift's journey correctly?

i

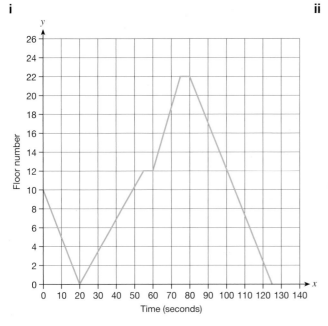

ii

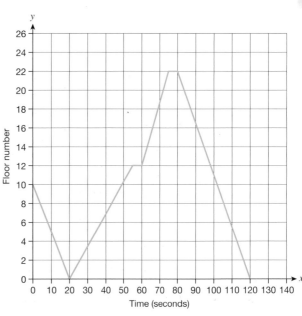

<table>
<tr><td>

This chapter is going to show you

- how to multiply and divide by 10, 100 and 1000
- how to round numbers to one decimal place
- how to use a calculator efficiently

</td><td>

What you should already know

- How to multiply and divide by 10
- How to round to the nearest 10 and 100
- How to use standard column methods for the four operations

</td></tr>
</table>

Rounding

The nearest star, Proxima Centauri, is 40 653 234 200 000 kilometres from earth. An atom is 0.000 000 0001 metres wide. When dealing with very large and very small numbers it is easier to round them and to work with powers of 10. You will meet this later when you do work on Standard Form. In this section you will round numbers, and multiply and divide by powers of 10.

Example 8.1 Multiply each of these.

    a 0.937   **b** 2.363

    by **i** 10   **ii** 100   **iii** 1000

    a **i** $0.937 \times 10 = 9.37$

        ii $0.937 \times 100 = 93.7$

        iii $0.937 \times 1000 = 937$

    b **i** $2.363 \times 10 = 23.63$

        ii $2.363 \times 100 = 236.3$

        iii $2.363 \times 1000 = 2363$

Example 8.2 Divide each of these:

    a 6   **b** 50

    by **i** 10   **ii** 100

    a **i** $6 \div 10 = 0.6$

        ii $6 \div 100 = 0.06$

    b **i** $50 \div 10 = 5$

        ii $50 \div 100 = 0.5$

Example 8.3 Round each of these numbers to one decimal place (1 dp).

   a 9.35   **b** 4.323   **c** 5.99

   a 9.35 is 9.4 to 1 dp.   **b** 4.323 is 4.3 to 1 dp.   **c** 5.99 is 6.0 to 1 dp.

Exercise 8A

1 Round each of these numbers to one decimal place.

   a 4.722   **b** 3.097   **c** 2.634   **d** 1.932   **e** 0.784
   f 0.992   **g** 3.999   **h** 2.604   **i** 3.185   **j** 3.475

2 Round each of these numbers to   **i** the nearest whole number   **ii** one decimal place.

   a 4.72   **b** 3.07   **c** 2.634   **d** 1.932   **e** 0.78   **f** 0.92
   g 3.92   **h** 2.64   **i** 3.18   **j** 3.475   **k** 1.45   **l** 1.863

3 Multiply each of these numbers by   **i** 10   **ii** 100   **iii** 1000.

   a 5.3   **b** 0.79   **c** 24   **d** 5.063   **e** 0.003

4 Divide each of these numbers by   **i** 10 and   **ii** 100.

   a 83   **b** 4.1   **c** 457   **d** 6.04   **e** 34 781

5 Write down the answers to each of these.

   a 3.1×10 **b** 6.78×100 **c** 0.56×1000 **d** $34 \div 100$
   e $823 \div 100$ **f** $9.06 \div 10$ **g** 57.89×100 **h** $57.89 \div 100$
   i 0.038×1000 **j** $0.038 \div 10$ **k** 0.05×1000 **l** $543 \div 100$

Extension Work

Sometimes we need to round numbers to two decimal places. An obvious case is when we work with money. Here are two examples of rounding to two decimal places (2 dp):

5.642 becomes 5.64 to 2 dp; 8.776 becomes 8.78 to 2 dp.

Round each of these numbers to two decimal places.

   a 4.722   **b** 3.097   **c** 2.634   **d** 1.932   **e** 0.784
   f 0.992   **g** 3.999   **h** 2.604   **i** 3.185   **j** 3.475

Large numbers

Example 8.4

	10^6	10^5	10^4	10^3	10^2	10	1
a			5	8	7	0	2
b	1	7	0	0	0	5	6

Write down the two numbers shown in the diagram on the left in words. Consider each number in blocks of three digits, that is:

           58 702
        1 700 056

   a 58 702 = Fifty-eight thousand, seven hundred and two.

   b 1 700 056 = One million, seven-hundred thousand, and fifty-six.

Example 8.5

a The bar chart shows the annual profits for a large company over the previous five years. Estimate the profit for each year.

b The company chairman says: 'Profit in 2002 was nearly 50 million pounds.' Is the chairman correct?

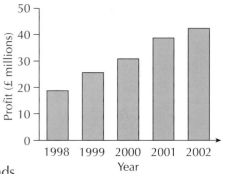

a In 1998 the profit was about 19 million pounds.
In 1999 it was about 25 million pounds.
In 2000 it was about 31 million pounds.
In 2001 it was about 39 million pounds.
In 2002 it was about 43 million pounds.

b The chairman is wrong, as in 2002 the profit is nearer 40 million pounds.

Exercise 8B

1 Write each of the following numbers in words.

a 4561	**b** 8009	**c** 56 430	**d** 22 108
e 60 092	**f** 302 999	**g** 306 708	**h** 213 045
i 3 452 763	**j** 2 047 809	**k** 12 008 907	**l** 3 006 098

2 Write each of the following numbers using figures.

a Six thousand, seven hundred and three.

b Twenty-one thousand and forty five.

c Two hundred and three thousand, four hundred and seventeen.

d Four million, forty-three thousand, two hundred and seven

e Nineteen million, five hundred and two thousand and thirty-seven

f One million, three hundred and two thousand and seven

3 The bar chart shows the population of some countries in the European Community. Estimate the population of each country.

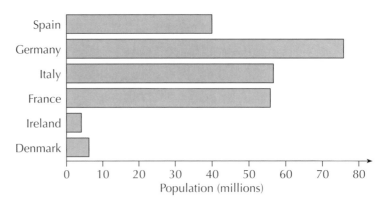

4 Round off each of the following numbers to **i** the nearest thousand, **ii** the nearest ten thousand and **iii** the nearest million.

a 3 547 812	**b** 9 722 106	**c** 3 042 309	**d** 15 698 999

5 There are 2 452 800 people out of work. The government says: 'Unemployment is just over two million.' The opposition says: 'Unemployment is still nearly three million.' Who is correct and why?

Extension Work

The diagram on the right shows a calculator display.

$$6.4^{03}$$

This means $6.4 \times 10^3 = 6.4 \times 1000 = 6400$

What number does each of the following calculator displays show?

a $\quad 2.4^{02}$ b $\quad 3.6^{02}$ c $\quad 7.8^{03}$ d $\quad 8.2^{03}$

Estimations

You should have an idea if the answer to a calculation is about the right size or not. Here are some ways of checking answers.

- First, when it is a multiplication, you can check that the final digit is correct.
- Second, you can round off numbers and do a mental calculation to see if an answer is about the right size.
- Third, you can check by doing the inverse operation.

Example 8.6

Explain why these calculations must be wrong.

a $\quad 23 \times 45 = 1053$ b $\quad 19 \times 59 = 121$

a The last digit should be 5, because the product of the last digits is 15. That is, $23 \times 45 = \ldots 5$

b The answer is roughly $20 \times 60 = 1200$.

Example 8.7

Estimate the answers to each of these calculations.

a $\quad \dfrac{21.3 + 48.7}{6.4}$ b $\quad 31.2 \times 48.5$ c $\quad 359 \div 42$

a Round the numbers on the top to $20 + 50 = 70$. Round off 6.4 to 7. Then $70 \div 7 = 10$.

b Round to 30×50, which is $3 \times 5 \times 100 = 1500$.

c Round to $360 \div 40$, which is $36 \div 4 = 9$.

Example 8.8

By using the inverse operation, check if each calculation is correct.

a $\quad 450 \div 6 = 75$ b $\quad 310 - 59 = 249$

a By the inverse operation, $450 = 6 \times 75$. This is true and can be checked mentally: $6 \times 70 = 420$, $6 \times 5 = 30$, $420 + 30 = 450$.

b By the inverse operation, $310 = 249 + 59$. This addition must end in 8 as $9 + 9 = 18$, so the calculation cannot be correct.

Example 8.9 Estimate the answers to:

    a   12% of 923
    b $\dfrac{11.2 + 53.6}{18.7 - 9.6}$
    c $324 \div 59$

    a   Round to   10% of 900 = 90

    b   Round to $\dfrac{10 + 50}{20 - 10} = \dfrac{60}{10} = 6$

    c   Round to $300 \div 60 = 5$

Exercise 8C

1   Explain why these calculations must be wrong.

    a $24 \times 42 = 1080$
    b $51 \times 73 = 723$
    c $\dfrac{34.5 + 63.2}{9.7} = 20.07$

    d $360 \div 8 = 35$
    e $354 - 37 = 323$

2   Estimate the answer to each of these problems.

    a $2768 - 392$
    b 231×18
    c $792 \div 38$
    d $\dfrac{36.7 + 23.2}{14.1}$

    e 423×423
    f $157.2 \div 38.2$
    g $\dfrac{135.7 - 68.2}{15.8 - 8.9}$
    h $\dfrac{38.9 \times 61.2}{39.6 - 18.4}$

3   Delroy had £10. In his shopping basket he had a magazine costing £2.65, some batteries costing £1.92, and a tape costing £4.99. Without adding up the numbers, how could Delroy be sure he had enough to buy the goods in the basket? Explain a quick way for Delroy to find out if he could afford a 45p bar of chocolate as well.

4   Amy bought 6 bottles of pop at 46p per bottle. The shopkeeper asked her for £3.16. Without working out the correct answer, explain why this is wrong.

5   A first class stamp is 27p. I need eight. Will £2 be enough to pay for them? Explain your answer clearly.

6   In a shop I bought a 53p comic and a £1.47 model car. The till said £54.47. Why?

7   Estimate the value the arrow is pointing at in each of these:

    a   0.7   3.7

    b   0   6.3

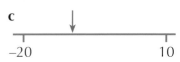
    c   −20   10

8   Estimate the answers to:

    a   23% of 498
    b 6.72^2
    c 523×69
    d $\frac{1}{3}$ of 320

    e 1.75×16
    f 287×102
    g $\dfrac{18.3 - 5.2}{10.7 + 8.6}$
    h $\dfrac{178 \times 18}{21}$

Extension Work

Without working out areas or counting squares, explain why the area of the square shown must be between 36 and 64 grid squares.

    a   Now calculate the area of the square.

    b   Using an 8 × 8 grid, draw a square with an area of exactly 50 grid squares.

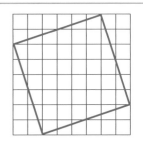

Adding and subtracting decimals

Example 8.10

Work out:

a   64.06 + 178.9 + 98.27   b   20 − 8.72 − 6.5

The numbers need to be lined up in columns with their decimal points in line.
Blank places are filled with zeros. Part **b** needs to be done in two stages.

a
```
    64.06
   178.90
 +  98.27
   341.23
     2 1  1
```

b
```
   1 9 9 1
   2̶0̶.0̶0̶       0 1
              1̶1̶.28
 −  8.72    −  6.50
   11.28      4.78
```

Example 8.11

In a science lesson, a student adds 0.45 kg of water and 0.72 kg of salt to a beaker
that weighs 0.09 kg. He then pours out 0.6 kg of the mixture. What is the total mass
of the beaker and mixture remaining?

This has to be set up as an addition and subtraction problem. That is:

0.09 + 0.45 + 0.72 − 0.6

The problem has to be done in two stages:

```
   0.09       0 1
   0.45       1̶.26
 + 0.72     − 0.60
   1.26       0.66
    1  1
```

So the final mass is 0.66 kg or 660 grams.

Exercise 8D

1 Work out each of the following.

a   4.32 + 65.09 + 172.3   b   8.7 + 9 + 14.02 + 1.03

c   11.42 + 15.72 − 12.98   d   42.7 + 67.3 − 35.27

e   19.87 + 2.8 − 13.46   f   12 − 5.09 + 3.21

g   23.9 + 8 − 9.25   h   7.05 + 2.9 + 7 + 0.64

i   7.25 + 19.3 − 12.06

j   21.35 + 6.72 − 12.36 − 5.71

2 There are 1000 metres in a kilometre. Calculate each of the following (work in
kilometres).

a   7.45 km + 843 m + 68 m

b   3.896 km + 723 m + 92 m

c   8.76 km + 463 m − 892 m

d   16 km − 435 m − 689 m

e   7.8 km + 5.043 km − 989 m

3 There are 1000 grams in a kilogram. Calculate the mass of each of the following shopping baskets (work in kilograms).

    a 3.2 kg of apples, 454 g of jam, 750 g of lentils, 1.2 kg of flour.

    b 1.3 kg of sugar, 320 g of strawberries, 0.65 kg of rice.

4 In an experiment a beaker of water has a mass of 1.104 kg. The beaker alone weighs 0.125 kg. What is the mass of water in the beaker (in kilograms)?

5 A rectangle is 2.35 m by 43 cm. What is its perimeter (in metres)?

6 A piece of string is 5 m long. Pieces of length 84 cm, 1.23 m and 49 cm are cut from it. How much string is left (in metres)?

Extension Work

Centimetres and millimetres both show lengths. The first length shown on the rule below, AB, can be given as 1.6 cm, 16 mm or $1\frac{3}{5}$ cm.

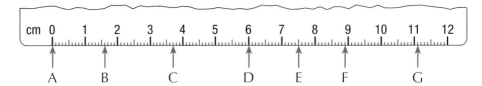

Write each length shown below
i in centimetres as a decimal   **ii** in millimetres   **iii** in centimetres as a fraction

a AC   **b** BD   **c** CE   **d** DE   **e** EF   **f** EG

Efficient calculations

You should have your own calculator, so that you can get used to it. Make sure that you understand how to use the basic functions ($\times$, $\div$, $+$, $-$) and the square, square root and brackets keys. They are different even on scientific calculators.

Example 8.12

Use a calculator to work out **a** $\dfrac{242 + 118}{88 - 72}$ **b** $\dfrac{63 \times 224}{32 \times 36}$

The line that separates the top numbers from the bottom numbers acts both as a divide sign ($\div$) and as brackets.

a Key the calculation as $(242 + 118) \div (88 - 72) = 22.5$

b Key the calculation as $(63 \times 224) \div (32 \times 36) = 12.25$

Example 8.13

Use a calculator to work out **a** $\sqrt{1764}$ **b** 23.4^2 **c** $52.3 - (30.4 - 17.3)$

a Some calculators need the square root after the number has been keyed, some need it before: $\sqrt{1764} = 42$

b Most calculators have a special key for squaring: $23.4^2 = 547.56$

c This can be keyed in exactly as it reads: $52.3 - (30.4 - 17.3) = 39.2$

1 Without using a calculator, work out the value of each of these.

a $\dfrac{17 + 8}{7 - 2}$ **b** $\dfrac{53 - 8}{3.5 - 2}$ **c** $\dfrac{19.2 - 1.7}{5.6 - 3.1}$

2 Use a calculator to do the calculations in Question 1. Do you get the same answers?
For each part, write down the sequence of keys that you pressed to get the answer.

3 Work out the value of each of these. Round off your answers to 1 dp if necessary.

a $\dfrac{194 + 866}{122 + 90}$ **b** $\dfrac{213 + 73}{63 - 19}$ **c** $\dfrac{132 + 88}{78 - 28}$ **d** $\dfrac{792 + 88}{54 - 21}$

e $\dfrac{790 \times 84}{24 \times 28}$ **f** $\dfrac{642 \times 24}{87 - 15}$ **g** $\dfrac{107 + 853}{24 \times 16}$ **h** $\dfrac{57 - 23}{18 - 7.8}$

4 Estimate the answer to $\dfrac{231 + 167}{78 - 32}$

Now use a calculator to work out the answer to 1 dp. Is it about the same?

5 Work out each of these.

a $\sqrt{42.25}$ **b** $\sqrt{68.89}$ **c** 2.6^2 **d** 3.9^2

e $\sqrt{(23.8 + 66.45)}$ **f** $\sqrt{(7 - 5.04)}$ **g** $(5.2 - 1.8)^2$ **h** $(2.5 + 6.1)^2$

6 Work out

a $8.3 - (4.2 - 1.9)$ **b** $12.3 + (3.2 - 1.7)^2$ **c** $(3.2 + 1.9)^2 - (5.2 - 2.1)^2$

7 Use a calculator to find the quotient and the remainder when

a 985 is divided by 23 **b** 802 is divided by 36

8 A calculator shows an answer of

2.33333333333

Write this as a mixed number or a top heavy fraction.

Extension Work

On your calculator you may have a key or a function above a key marked $x!$.

Find out what this key does. For example, on some calculators you can key:

3 $x!$ and the display shows 6,

and you can key:

7 $x!$ and the display shows 5040.

Similarly, investigate what the key marked $1/x$ or x^{-1} does.

Long multiplication and long division

Example 8.14 Work out 36 × 43.

Below are four examples of the ways this calculation can be done. The answer is 1548.

Box method (partitioning)	Column method (expanded working)	Column method (compacted working)	Chinese method

Box method (partitioning):

×	30	6	
40	1200	240	1440
3	90	18	108
			1548

Column method (expanded working):
```
     36
 ×   43
     18   (3 × 6)
     90   (3 × 30)
    240   (40 × 6)
   1200   (40 × 30)
   1548
```

Column method (compacted working):
```
     36
 ×   43
    108   (3 × 36)
   1440   (40 × 36)
   1548
```

Chinese method:

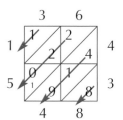

Example 8.15 Work out 543 ÷ 31.

Below are two examples of the ways this can be done. The answer is 17, remainder 16.

Subtracting multiples
```
   543
 - 310   (10 × 31)
   233
 - 155   (5 × 31)
    78
 -  62   (2 × 31)
    16
```

Traditional method
```
         17
   31 / 543
         31
        233
        217
         16
```

Exercise 8F

1 Work out each of the following long multiplication problems. Use any method you are happy with.

   a 17 × 23   **b** 32 × 42   **c** 19 × 45   **d** 56 × 46

   e 12 × 346   **f** 32 × 541   **g** 27 × 147   **h** 39 × 213

2 Work out each of the following long division problems. Use any method you are happy with. Some of the problems will have a remainder.

   a 684 ÷ 19   **b** 966 ÷ 23   **c** 972 ÷ 36   **d** 625 ÷ 25

   e 930 ÷ 38   **f** 642 ÷ 24   **g** 950 ÷ 33   **h** 800 ÷ 42

Decide whether each of the following nine problems involves long multiplication or long division. Then do the appropriate calculation, showing your method clearly.

3 Each day 17 Jumbo jets fly from London to San Francisco. Each jet can carry up to 348 passengers. How many people can travel from London to San Francisco each day?

4 A company has 897 boxes to move by van. The van can carry 23 boxes at a time. How many trips must the van make to move all the boxes?

5 The same van does 34 miles to a gallon of petrol. How many miles can it do if the petrol tank holds 18 gallons?

6 The school photocopier can print 82 sheets a minute. If it runs without stopping for 45 minutes, how many sheets will it print?

7 The RE department has printed 525 sheets on Buddhism. These are put into folders in sets of 35. How many folders are there?

8 a To raise money, Wath Running Club are going to do a relay race from Wath to Edinburgh, which is 384 kilometres. Each runner will run 24 kilometres. How many runners will be needed to cover the distance?

b Sponsorship will bring in £32 per kilometre. How much money will the club raise?

9 Computer floppy disks are 45p each. How much will a box of 35 disks cost. Give your answer in pounds.

10 The daily newspaper sells advertising by the square inch. On Monday, it sells 232 square inches at £15 per square inch. How much money does it get from this advertising?

11 The local library has 13 000 books. Each shelf holds 52 books. How many shelves are there?

12 How many bubble packs of 48 nails can be filled from a carton of 400 nails?

Extension Work

The box method can be used to do decimal multiplications. For example,
2.5×4.8 can be worked out as follows.

×	4	0.8	Sum of row
2	8	1.6	9.6
0.5	2	0.4	2.4
		Total	12.0

Use the box method to calculate 1.4×2.4.

Check your answer with a calculator.

What you need to know for level 4

- How to add and subtract decimals with up to two decimal places
- How to round numbers to the nearest 10, 100 and 1000

What you need to know for level 5

- How to round numbers to one decimal place
- How to use the bracket, square, square root and sign-change keys on your calculator
- How to make estimations of calculations
- How to multiply and divide a three-digit whole number by a two-digit whole number

National Curriculum SATs questions

LEVEL 4

1   *1999 Paper 2*

Here are some number cards. $\boxed{1}$ $\boxed{7}$ $\boxed{3}$ $\boxed{5}$

Use some of the four cards to make numbers that are as close as possible to the numbers shown.

For example: 80 → $\boxed{7}$ $\boxed{5}$, 30 → $\boxed{3}$ $\boxed{1}$

50 →   60 →   4000 →   1500 →   1600 →

2   *1998 Paper 2*

The table shows the lengths of some rivers to the nearest km.

River	Severn	Thames	Trent	Wye	Dee
Length	354	346	297	215	113

a   Write the length of each river rounded to the nearest 100 km. Which two rivers have the same length to the nearest 100 km?

b   Write the length of each river rounded to the nearest 10 km. Which two rivers have the same length to the nearest 10 km?

c   There is a river that is not on the list. It has a length of 200 km to the nearest 100 km and a length of 150 km to the nearest 10 km. Give one possible length of the river to the nearest km.

d   Two more rivers have different lengths to the nearest km. They both have a length of 250 km to the nearest 10 km, but their lengths to the nearest 100 km are different. Give a possible length of each river to the nearest km.

LEVEL 5

3 *2001 Paper 1*

    a A football club is planning a trip. The club hires 234 coaches. Each coach holds 52 passengers. How many passengers is that altogether?

    b The club wants to put one first aid kit into each of the 234 coaches. The first aid kits are sold in boxes of 18. How many boxes does the club need?

4 *2002 Paper 1*

    a Peter's height is 0.9 m. Lucy is 0.3 m taller than Peter. What is Lucy's height?

    b Lee's height is 1.45 m. Misha is 0.3 m shorter than Lee. What is Misha's height?

    c Zita's height is 1.7 m. What is Zita's height in centimetres?

CHAPTER 9 Shape, Space and Measures **3**

This chapter is going to show you

- how to recognise congruent shapes
- how to transform 2-D shapes by combinations of reflections, rotations and translations
- how to solve problems using ratio

What you should already know

- How to reflect a 2-D shape in a mirror line
- How to rotate a 2-D shape about a point
- How to translate a 2-D shape
- How to use ratio

Congruent shapes

All the triangles on the grid below are reflections, rotations or translations of Triangle A. What do you notice about them?

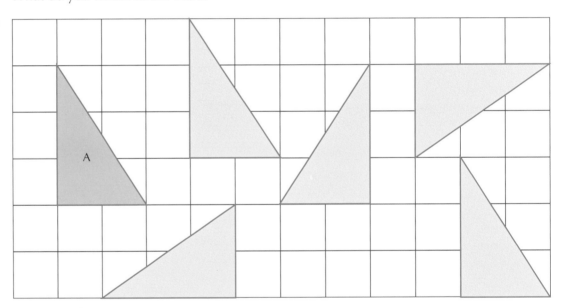

You should remember that the image triangles are exactly the same shape and size as the object Triangle A.

Two shapes are said to be **congruent** if they are exactly the same shape and size. Reflections, rotations and translations all produce images that are congruent to the original object. For shapes that are congruent, all the corresponding sides and angles are equal.

Example 9.1 ▷ Which two shapes below are congruent?

Shapes **b** and **d** are exactly the same shape and size, so **b** and **d** are congruent.
Tracing paper can be used to check that two shapes are congruent.

Exercise 9A

1 For each pair of shapes below, state whether they are congruent or not (use tracing paper to help if you are not sure).

  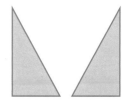

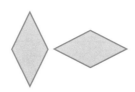 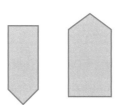 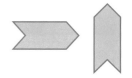

2 Which pairs of shapes on the grid below are congruent?

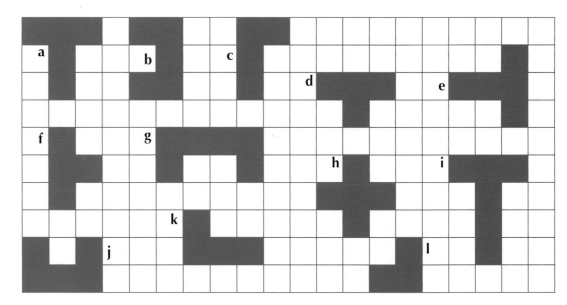

3 Which of the shapes below are congruent?

a 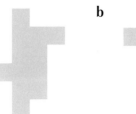　　b 　　c 　　d

4 Two congruent right-angled triangles are placed together with two of their equal sides touching to make another shape, as shown on the diagram below:

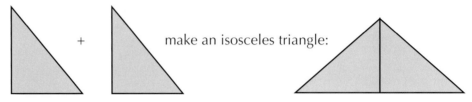

　　+　　make an isosceles triangle:

    a How many different shapes can you make? To help, you can cut out the triangles from a piece of card.

    b Repeat the activity using two congruent isosceles triangles.

    c Repeat the activity using two congruent equilateral triangles.

Extension Work

The 4-by-4 pinboard is divided into two congruent shapes:

Use square-dotted paper to show the number of different ways this can be done.

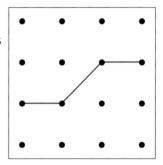

Combinations of transformations

The three single transformations you have met so far and the notation that we use to explain these transformations are shown below.

Reflections　　Mirror line

Triangle ABC is mapped onto triangle A'B'C' by a reflection in the mirror line. The object and the image are congruent.

Rotations

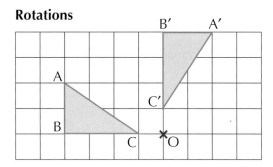

Triangle ABC is mapped onto triangle A′B′C′ by a rotation of 90° clockwise about the centre of rotation O. The object and the image are congruent.

Translations

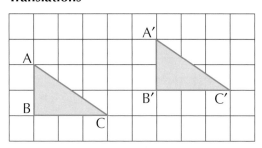

Triangle ABC is mapped onto triangle A′B′C′ by a translation of five units to the right, followed by one unit up. The object and the image are congruent.

The example below shows how a shape can be transformed by a combination of two of the above transformations.

Example 9.2

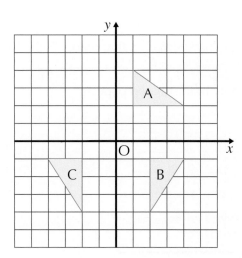

Triangle A is mapped onto triangle C after two combined transformations. Firstly, a rotation of 90° clockwise about the origin O maps A onto B. Secondly a reflection in the y-axis maps B onto C.

So, Triangle A is mapped onto Triangle C by a rotation of 90° clockwise about the origin O, followed by a reflection in the y-axis.

Exercise 9B

Tracing paper and a mirror will be useful for this exercise.

1 Copy the diagram below onto squared paper.

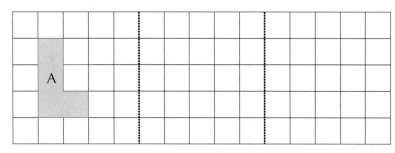

Mirror line 1   Mirror line 2

a Reflect shape A in mirror line 1 to give shape B.

b Reflect shape B in mirror line 2 to give shape C.

c Describe the single transformation that maps shape A onto shape C.

2 Copy the diagram below onto squared paper:

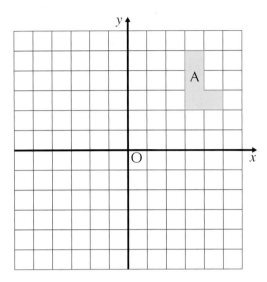

a Reflect shape A in the *x*-axis to give shape B.

b Reflect shape B in the *y*-axis to give shape C.

c Describe the single transformation that maps shape A onto shape C.

3 Copy the diagram below onto squared paper:

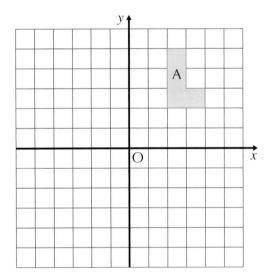

a Rotate shape A 90° clockwise about the origin O to give shape B.

b Rotate shape B 90° clockwise about the origin O to give shape C.

c Describe the single transformation that maps shape A onto shape C.

4 Copy the diagram below onto squared paper:

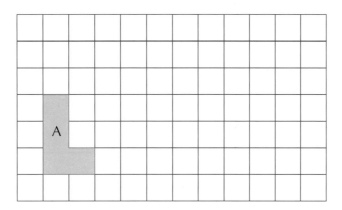

a Translate shape A three units to the right, followed by two units up, to give shape B.

b Translate shape B four units to the right, followed by 1 unit down, to give shape C.

c Describe the single transformation that maps shape A onto shape C.

5 Copy the triangles A, B, C, D, E and F onto a square grid, as shown:

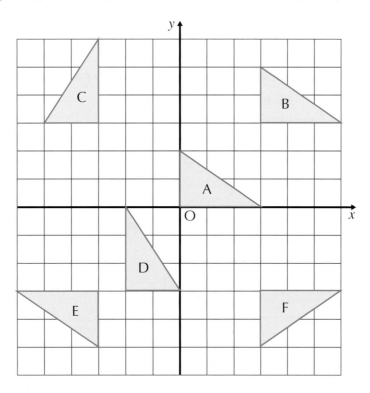

a Find a single transformation that will map:
  i A onto B   **ii** E onto F   **iii** B onto E   **iv** C onto B

b Find a combination of two transformations that will map:
  i A onto C   **ii** B onto F   **iii** F onto D   **iv** B onto E

1 Copy the congruent 'T' shapes A, B, C and D onto a square grid, as shown.

Find a combination of two transformations that will map:

   a   A onto B   **b**   A onto C

   c   A onto D   **d**   B onto C

   e   B onto D   **f**   C onto D

2 Use ICT software, such as LOGO, to transform shapes by using various combinations of reflections, rotations and translations. Print out some examples and present them on a poster.

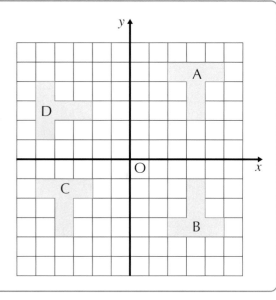

Reflections in two mirror lines

A shape can be reflected in two perpendicular mirror lines as the example below shows.

Example 9.3 ▷ Reflect the 'L' Shape in mirror line 1, then in mirror line 2.

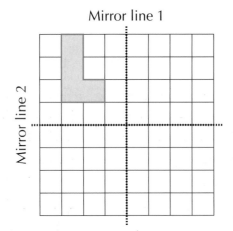

Reflecting in mirror line 1 gives:

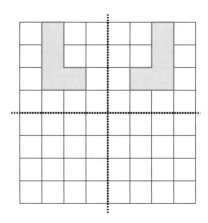

Reflecting both shapes in mirror line 2 gives:

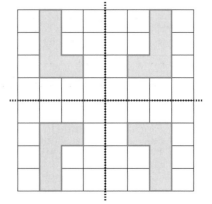

1 Copy each of the following shapes on to centimetre-squared paper and reflect it in both mirror lines shown.

a

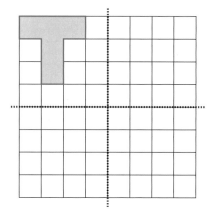

b

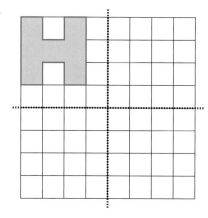

c

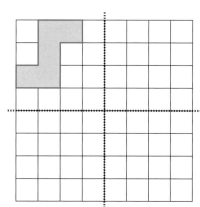

d

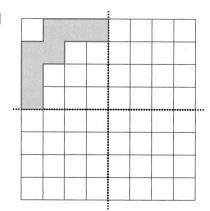

2 Copy each of the following diagrams on to centimetre-squared paper and reflect the shape in both mirror lines.

a

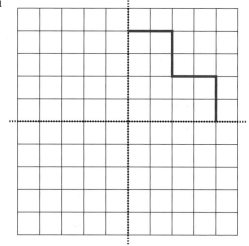

b

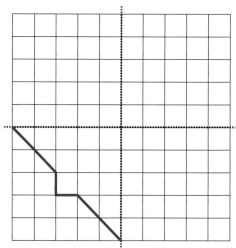

1   Copy the diagram below on to centimetre-squared paper and reflect the shape in the two diagonal mirror lines.

2   Make up some of your own examples to show how a shape can be reflected in two diagonal lines.

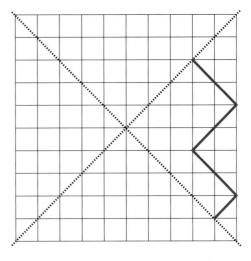

Shape and ratio

Ratio can be used to compare lengths and areas of 2-D shapes, as the following examples show.

Example 9.4

A ———— B   C ═══════════════════ D
  12 mm   4.8 cm

To find the ratio of the length of the line segment AB to the length of the line segment CD, change the measurements to the smallest unit and then simplify the ratio. So the ratio is 12 mm : 4.8 cm = 12 mm : 48 mm = 1 : 4. Remember that ratios have no units in the final answer.

Example 9.5

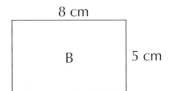

Find the ratio of the area of rectangle A to the area of rectangle B, giving the answer in its simplest form.

The ratio is 12 cm² : 40 cm² = 3 : 10.

Exercise 9D

① Express each of the following ratios in its simplest form.

a   10 mm : 25 mm   **b**   2 mm : 2 cm   **c**   36 cm : 45 cm

d   40 cm : 2 m   **e**   500 m : 2 km

2 For the two squares shown, find each of the following ratios, giving your answers in their simplest form:

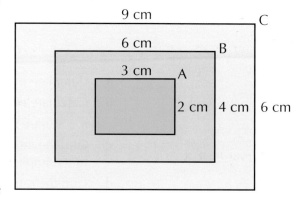

6 cm

2 cm

A   2 cm

B   6 cm

a The length of a side of square A to the length of a side of square B.

b The perimeter of square A to the perimeter of square B.

c The area of square A to the area of square B.

3 Three rectangles A, B and C are arranged as in the diagram. The ratio of the length of A to the length of B to the length of C is 3 cm : 6 cm : 9 cm = 1 : 2 : 3.

a Find each of the following ratios in the same way, giving your answers in their simplest form:

i The width of A to the width of B to the width of C.

ii The perimeter of A to the perimeter of B to the perimeter of C.

iii The area of A to the area of B to the area of C.

b Write down anything you notice about the three rectangles.

9 cm   C

6 cm   B

3 cm   A

2 cm | 4 cm | 6 cm

4 In the diagram, Flag X is mapped onto Flag Y by a reflection in mirror line 1. Flag X is also mapped onto Flag Z by a reflection in mirror line 2.

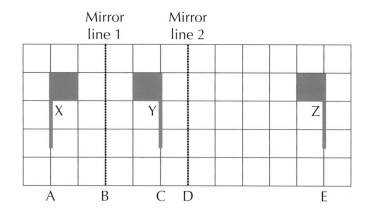

Mirror line 1   Mirror line 2

X   Y   Z

A   B   C   D   E

Find the ratio of each of the following lengths, giving your answers in their simplest form:

a AB : BC   **b** AB : AE   **c** AC : AE   **d** BD : CE

5 a Find the ratio of the area of the pink square to the area of the yellow surround, giving your answer in its simplest form.

b Express the area of the pink square as a fraction of the area of the yellow surround.

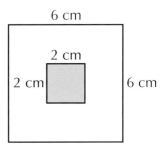

6 The dimensions of lawn A and lawn B are given on the diagrams.

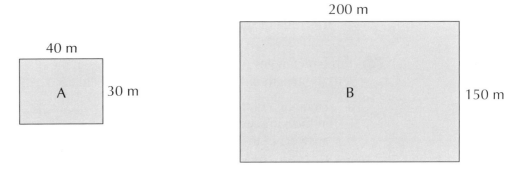

a Calculate the area of lawn A, giving your answer in square metres.

b Calculate the area of lawn B giving your answer in:

   i square meters   **ii** hectares (1 hectare = 10 000 m²)

c Find the ratio of the length of lawn A to the length of lawn B, giving your answer in its simplest form.

d Find the ratio of the area of lawn A to the area of lawn B, giving your answer in its simplest form.

e Express the area of lawn A as a fraction of the area of lawn B.

Extension Work

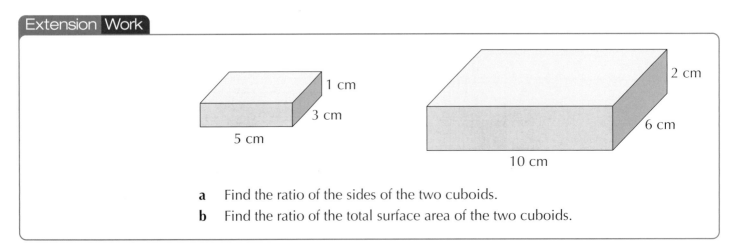

a Find the ratio of the sides of the two cuboids.

b Find the ratio of the total surface area of the two cuboids.

What you need to know for level 5
- How to recognise congruent shapes
- How to recognise and visualise simple transformations of 2-D shapes
- How to solve problems using ratio

National Curriculum SATs questions

LEVEL 4

1 *1997 Paper 1*

Some board games have pegs in holes.

a Copy the patterns on to square dotted paper and shade 5 more pegs so that the dashed line is a line of symmetry.

You may use a mirror or tracing paper to help.

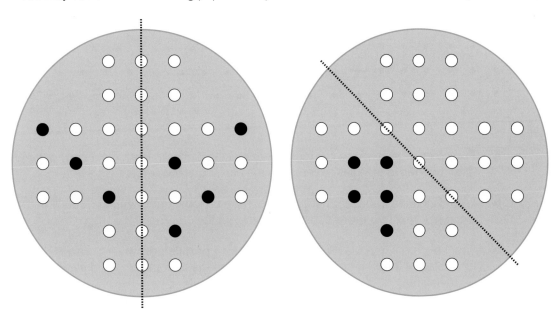

b Shade 9 more pegs so that both dashed lines are lines of symmetry.

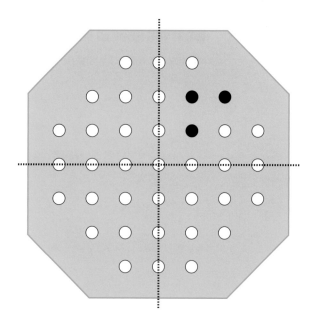

LEVEL 5

2 *2002 Paper 1*

Four squares join together to make a bigger square.

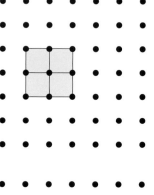

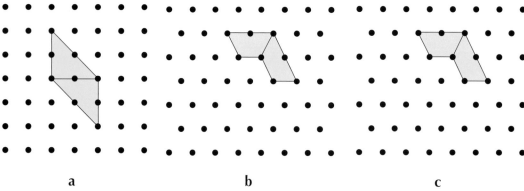

  a   **b**   **c**

a **Four** congruent triangles join together to make a bigger triangle. On a copy of the diagram, draw **two more** triangles to complete the drawing of the bigger triangle.

b Four congruent trapezia join together to make a bigger trapezium. On a copy of the diagram, draw **two more** trapezia to complete the drawing of the bigger trapezium.

c Four congruent trapezia join together to make a **parallelogram**. On a copy of the diagram, draw **two more** trapezia to complete the drawing of the parallelogram.

3 *1999 Paper 2*

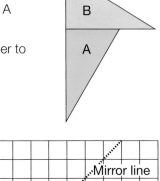

    a   Copy the diagram onto squared paper. You can rotate triangle A onto triangle B.

         Put a cross on the centre of rotation. You may use tracing paper to help you.

    b   You can rotate triangle A onto triangle B. The rotation is anti-clockwise. What is the angle of rotation?

    c   Copy the diagram onto squared paper. Reflect triangle A in the mirror line. You may use a mirror or tracing paper to help you.

Mirror line

A

4 *1999 Paper 2*

    a   Nigel pours 1 carton of apple juice and 3 cartons of orange juice into a big jug. What is the ratio of apple juice to orange juice in Nigel's jug?

    b   Lesley pours 1 carton of apple juice and $1\frac{1}{2}$ cartons of orange juice into another big jug. What is the ratio of apple juice to orange juice in Lesley's jug?

    c   Tandi pours 1 carton of apple juice and 1 carton of orange juice into another big jug. She wants only half as much apple juice as orange juice in her jug. What should Tandi pour into her jug now?

CHAPTER 10

Algebra 4

This chapter is going to show you

- how to solve more difficult equations
- how to substitute into a formula
- how to create your own expressions and formulae

What you should already know

- How to add, subtract and multiply negative numbers

Puzzle mappings

The mappings you are going to meet will contain an unknown value, often written as x. This is called the **unknown** of the mapping. The puzzle is to find the value of x, which you will do by **inverse mapping**.

Example 10.1 ▷ Find the value of x in the mapping

$$x \longrightarrow \boxed{\times 3} \longrightarrow 12$$

The inverse of $\times 3$ is $\div 3$. So, use the inverse mapping:

$$4 \longleftarrow \boxed{\div 3} \longleftarrow 12$$

which gives $x = 4$.

Example 10.2 ▷ Find the value of A in the mapping

$$A \longrightarrow \boxed{+ 5} \longrightarrow 16$$

The inverse of $+ 5$ is $- 5$. So, use the inverse mapping:

$$11 \longleftarrow \boxed{- 5} \longleftarrow 16$$

which gives $A = 11$.

Exercise 10A

1. Find the unknown in each of these mappings.

   a $x \longrightarrow \boxed{+ 3} \longrightarrow 17$ **b** $y \longrightarrow \boxed{\times 4} \longrightarrow 20$ **c** $p \longrightarrow \boxed{- 2} \longrightarrow 8$

   d $q \longrightarrow \boxed{\times 2} \longrightarrow 16$ **e** $t \longrightarrow \boxed{+ 5} \longrightarrow 19$ **f** $m \longrightarrow \boxed{- 3} \longrightarrow 12$

   g $A \longrightarrow \boxed{+ 7} \longrightarrow 20$ **h** $B \longrightarrow \boxed{- 4} \longrightarrow 5$ **i** $p \longrightarrow \boxed{\times 5} \longrightarrow 15$

2 A teacher put some puzzle mappings on the board. Someone rubbed out parts of each problem. Copy and complete each mapping.

a $x \longrightarrow \boxed{} \longrightarrow 9$

$\longleftarrow \boxed{-4}$

$x =$

b $A \longrightarrow \boxed{} \longrightarrow$

$\longleftarrow \boxed{\div 2} \longleftarrow 12$

$A =$

c $y \longrightarrow \boxed{\times 3} \longrightarrow$

$\longleftarrow \boxed{} \longleftarrow 15$

$y =$

d $t \longrightarrow \boxed{} \longrightarrow 9$

$7 \longleftarrow \boxed{} \longleftarrow$

$t =$

e $m \longrightarrow \boxed{} \longrightarrow 2$

$5 \longleftarrow \boxed{} \longleftarrow$

$m =$

f $B \longrightarrow \boxed{-3} \longrightarrow 14$

$\longleftarrow \boxed{+3} \longleftarrow$

$B =$

3 Find the missing number in each of these.

a $3 + \boxed{} = 11$

b $4 \times \boxed{} = 12$

c $10 - \boxed{} = 3$

d $5 \times \boxed{} = 30$

e $8 + \boxed{} = 12$

f $9 - \boxed{} = 7$

g $4 + \boxed{} = 15$

h $3 \times \boxed{} = 18$

i $12 - \boxed{} = 9$

j $6 \times \boxed{} = 18$

k $15 - \boxed{} = 9$

l $7 + \boxed{} = 15$

4 Solve each of the following equations.

a $x + 5 = 12$

b $2s = 10$

c $t + 3 = 12$

d $g - 5 = 12$

e $4x = 20$

f $4x = 12$

g $v + 9 = 39$

h $x - 3 = 11$

i $6x = 24$

j $q + 5 = 26$

k $5x = 35$

l $p - 8 = 17$

Extension Work

Using only whole positive numbers and 0, in how many different ways can you complete each of the following? Show all your answers.

a $\boxed{} + \boxed{} = 9$

b $\boxed{} \times \boxed{} = 24$

c $\boxed{} - \boxed{} = 7$

More puzzle mappings

All the puzzle mappings that you met in the last lesson had only one operation. This lesson will deal with puzzle mappings that have more than one operation.

Example 10.3

Find the value of x in the mapping.

$$x \longrightarrow \boxed{\times 5} \longrightarrow \boxed{+ 3} \longrightarrow 18$$

Put in the inverse of each operation and work backwards:

$$? \longleftarrow \boxed{\div 5} \longleftarrow \boxed{- 3} \longleftarrow 18$$
$$3 \longleftarrow 15 \longleftarrow 18$$

which gives $x = 3$.

Example 10.4

Find the value of y in the mapping

$$y \longrightarrow \boxed{+ 2} \longrightarrow \boxed{\div 3} \longrightarrow 18$$

Put in the inverse of each operation and work backwards:

$$? \longleftarrow \boxed{- 2} \longleftarrow \boxed{\div 3} \longleftarrow 18$$
$$4 \longleftarrow 6 \longleftarrow 18$$

which gives $y = 4$.

Exercise 10B

1 Use inverse mapping to find the value of x in each of the following.

a $\quad x \longrightarrow \boxed{\times 2} \longrightarrow \boxed{+ 3} \longrightarrow 13$ b $\quad x \longrightarrow \boxed{\times 3} \longrightarrow \boxed{+ 5} \longrightarrow 11$

c $\quad x \longrightarrow \boxed{\times 2} \longrightarrow \boxed{+ 9} \longrightarrow 17$ d $\quad x \longrightarrow \boxed{+ 1} \longrightarrow \boxed{\times 5} \longrightarrow 35$

e $\quad x \longrightarrow \boxed{+ 3} \longrightarrow \boxed{\times 4} \longrightarrow 16$ f $\quad x \longrightarrow \boxed{+ 2} \longrightarrow \boxed{\times 7} \longrightarrow 21$

g $\quad x \longrightarrow \boxed{\times 4} \longrightarrow \boxed{+ 5} \longrightarrow 29$ h $\quad x \longrightarrow \boxed{\times 5} \longrightarrow \boxed{+ 3} \longrightarrow 28$

i $\quad x \longrightarrow \boxed{\times 3} \longrightarrow \boxed{+ 4} \longrightarrow 25$ j $\quad x \longrightarrow \boxed{+ 2} \longrightarrow \boxed{\times 5} \longrightarrow 30$

2 Copy and complete the missing parts of each of these puzzle mappings.

a

$x =$

b
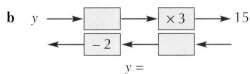
$y =$

c

$t =$

d
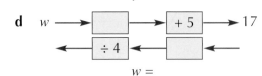
$w =$

e
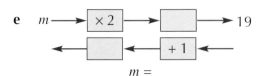
$m =$

f
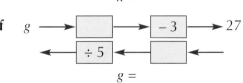
$g =$

3 Pete had a number rule in his head. He used the rule on any number given to him

> Multiply by 2.
> Then subtract 5.

  a What number did Pete give in reply to each of the following?

   i Mandy gave 7

   ii Paul gave 3

   iii Zahir gave 10.

  b What number was given to Peter when he replied as follows?

   i 19 to Ann   **ii** 9 to Steve   **iii** 21 to Alan

Extension Work

In how many different ways can you fill in the operation boxes in each of these mapping diagrams? Show all your answers.

a $2 \longrightarrow \boxed{} \longrightarrow \boxed{} \longrightarrow 20$

b $16 \longrightarrow \boxed{} \longrightarrow \boxed{} \longrightarrow 1$

Solving equations

An **equation** is formed when an expression is put equal to a number or another expression.

The equations you will meet contain only one unknown value, which is often represented by x. This is called the **unknown** of the equation. To find the value of the unknown, the equation has to be **solved**.

One way to solve equations is to use inverse mapping.

Example 10.5

Solve the equation $5x - 4 = 11$

The mapping which gives this equation is

$$x \longrightarrow \boxed{\times 5} \longrightarrow \boxed{-4} \longrightarrow 11$$

The inverse is

$$? \longleftarrow \boxed{\div 5} \longleftarrow \boxed{+4} \longleftarrow 11$$
$$3 \longleftarrow 15 \longleftarrow 11$$

which gives $x = 3$.

Example 10.6

Solve the equation $4x + 2 = 22$

The mapping which gives this equation is

$$x \longrightarrow \boxed{\times 4} \longrightarrow \boxed{+2} \longrightarrow 22$$

Working the mapping backwards:

   Subtract 2: $22 - 2 = 20$

   Divide by 4: $20 \div 4 = 5$

So, the solution is $x = 5$.

1 **i** Write the equation which is given by each of the following mapping.

   ii Use inverse mapping to solve each equation.

   a $x \longrightarrow \boxed{\times 2} \longrightarrow \boxed{+ 3} \longrightarrow 11$ **b** $x \longrightarrow \boxed{\times 3} \longrightarrow \boxed{+ 1} \longrightarrow 16$

   c $t \longrightarrow \boxed{\times 5} \longrightarrow \boxed{+ 4} \longrightarrow 34$ **d** $t \longrightarrow \boxed{\times 4} \longrightarrow \boxed{- 3} \longrightarrow 13$

   e $y \longrightarrow \boxed{\times 2} \longrightarrow \boxed{- 1} \longrightarrow 13$ **f** $y \longrightarrow \boxed{\times 7} \longrightarrow \boxed{+ 5} \longrightarrow 26$

2 **i** Write the mapping which is given by each of the following equations.

   ii Use inverse mapping to solve each equation.

   a $3x + 4 = 19$ **b** $2x + 5 = 11$ **c** $4x - 1 = 23$

   d $5x - 3 = 17$ **e** $3x + 1 = 22$ **f** $6x - 5 = 7$

3 Solve each of the following equations by first writing the inverse of the mapping given by the equation.

   a $2x + 3 = 15$ **b** $4x + 1 = 29$ **c** $3x + 4 = 25$

   d $5x - 1 = 34$ **e** $2x - 3 = 13$ **f** $4x - 3 = 37$

4 Solve each of the following equations.

   a $2x + 3 = 17$ **b** $4x - 1 = 19$ **c** $5x + 3 = 18$

   d $2y - 3 = 13$ **e** $4z + 5 = 17$ **f** $6x - 5 = 13$

   g $10b + 9 = 29$ **h** $2r - 3 = 9$ **i** $3x - 11 = 1$

   j $7p + 5 = 82$ **k** $5x + 7 = 52$ **l** $9x - 8 = 55$

Extension Work

$x \longrightarrow \boxed{\times 2} \longrightarrow \boxed{+ 1} \longrightarrow \boxed{\times 3} \longrightarrow y$

a Find the value of y when:

   i $x = 5$ **ii** $x = 4$ **iii** $x = 3$

b Find the value of x when:

   i $y = 39$ **ii** $y = 51$ **iii** $y = 57$

c Find the negative decimal value of x when $x \longrightarrow x$.

Substituting into expressions

Replacing the letters in an expression by numbers is called **substitution**.

Substituting different numbers will give an expression different values. You need to be able to substitute negative numbers as well as positive numbers into expressions.

Example 10.7 ▷   What is the value of $5x + 7$ when   **i** $x = 3$ **ii** $x = -1$.

   i When $x = 3$, $5x + 7 = 5 \times 3 + 7 = 22$

   ii When $x = -1$, $5x + 7 = 5 \times (-1) + 7 = -5 + 7 = 2$

1 Write down the value of each expression for each value of x.

		i		**ii**		**iii**	
a	$x + 3$	**i**	$x = 4$	**ii**	$x = 5$	**iii**	$x = -1$
b	$7 + x$	**i**	$x = 6$	**ii**	$x = 2$	**iii**	$x = -5$
c	$3x$	**i**	$x = 7$	**ii**	$x = 3$	**iii**	$x = -5$
d	$4x$	**i**	$x = 3$	**ii**	$x = 5$	**iii**	$x = -1$
e	$3x + 4$	**i**	$x = 5$	**ii**	$x = 4$	**iii**	$x = -2$
f	$5x - 1$	**i**	$x = 3$	**ii**	$x = 2$	**iii**	$x = -6$
g	$3x + 5$	**i**	$x = 3$	**ii**	$x = 7$	**iii**	$x = -1$
h	$4x + 20$	**i**	$x = 4$	**ii**	$x = 5$	**iii**	$x = -3$
i	$8 + 7x$	**i**	$x = 2$	**ii**	$x = 6$	**iii**	$x = -2$
j	$93 + 4x$	**i**	$x = 10$	**ii**	$x = 21$	**iii**	$x = -3$

2 If $a = 2$ and $b = 3$, find the value of each of the following.

    a $3a + b$ **b** $a + 3b$ **c** $3a + 5b$ **d** $4b - 3a)$

3 If $c = 5$ and $d = 2$, find the value of each of the following.

    a $2c + d$ **b** $6c - 2d$ **c** $3d + 7c$ **d** $3c - 5d$

4 If $e = 4$, $f = 3$ and $g = 2$, find the value of each of the following.

    a $ef + g$ **b** $eg - f$ **c** efg **d** $3e + 2f + 5g$

5 If $h = -4$, $j = 7$ and $k = 5$, find the value of each of the following.

    a hjk **b** $4k + fj$ **c** $5h + 4j + 3k$ **d** $3hj - 2hk$

Extension **Work**

1 What values of n can be substituted into n^2 that give n^2 a value less than 1?

2 What values of n can be substituted into $(n - 4)^2$ that give $(n - 4)^2$ a value less than 1?

3 What values of n can be substituted into $\frac{1}{n}$ that give $\frac{1}{n}$ a value less than 1?

4 Find at least five different expressions in x that give the value 10 when $x = 2$ is substituted into them.

Substituting into formulae

Formulae occur in all sorts of situations. A common example is the conversion between metric and imperial units.

Example 10.8

The formula for converting kilograms (K) to pounds weight (P) is:

$$P = 2.2K$$

Convert 10 kilograms to pounds weight.

Substituting $K = 10$ into the formula gives:

$$P = 2.2 \times 10 = 22$$

So, 10 kg is 22 pounds weight.

Example 10.9 ▷ The formula for the volume, V, of a box with length b, width w and height h, is given by

$$V = bwh$$

Calculate the volume of a box whose length is 8 cm, width is 3 cm and height is 2 cm.

Substitute the values given into the formula:

$$V = 8 \times 3 \times 2 = 48$$

So, the volume of the box is 48 cm³.

Exercise 10E

1. The area, A, of a rectangle is found using the formula $A = LB$, where L is its length and B its width. Find A when:

   i $L = 8$ and $B = 7$ ii $L = 6$ and $B = 1.5$

2. The surface area, A, of a coil is given by the formula $A = 6rh$. Find A when:

   i $r = 6$ and $h = 17$ ii $r = 2.5$ and $h = 12$

3. The sum, S, of the angles in a polygon with n sides is given by the formula $S = 180(n - 2)$. Find S when:

   i $n = 7$ ii $n = 12$

4. If $V = u + ft$, find V when

   i $u = 40, f = 32$ and $t = 5$ ii $u = 12, f = 13$ and $t = 10$

5. If $D = \frac{M}{V}$, find D when

   i $M = 28$ and $V = 4$ ii $M = 8$ and $V = 5$

6. A magician charges £25 for every show he performs, plus an extra £10 per hour spent on stage. The formula for calculating his charge is $C = 10t + 25$, where C is the charge in pounds and t is the length of the show in hours.

   How much does he charge for a show lasting

   i   1 hour ii   3 hours iii   2 hours?

7. The area (A) of the triangle shown is given by the formula $A = \frac{1}{2}bh$.

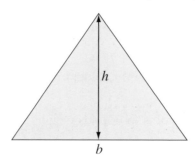

   Find the area when:

   i $h = 12$ cm and $b = 5$ cm ii $h = 9$ cm and $b = 8$ cm?

8 The following formula approximately converts temperatures in degrees Celsius (C) to degrees Fahrenheit (F).

$$F = 2C + 30$$

Convert approximately each of these temperatures to degrees Fahrenheit.

i 45 °C   **ii** 40 °C   **iii** 65 °C   **iv** 100 °C

9 The surface area (S) of this cuboid is given by the formula:

$$S = 2ab + 2bc + 2ac$$

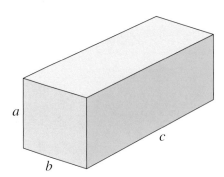

a Find the surface area, when $a = 3$ m, $b = 4$ m and $c = 5$ m.

b Find

  i the surface area when $a = 3$ cm, and a, b and c are all the same length.

  ii What name is given to this cuboid?

Extension Work

The triangle numbers are given by the following formula:

$$T = \frac{n(n + 1)}{2}$$

The first triangle number is found by substituting in $n = 1$, which gives

$$T = 1 \times \frac{(1 + 1)}{2} = 1$$

a Find the first five triangle numbers.

b Find the 99th triangle number.

Creating your own expressions and formulae

The last lesson showed you some formulae which could be used to solve problems. In this lesson, you will be given problems and have to write your own formulae to help solve them.

You will need to choose a letter to represent each variable in a problem, and use it when you write the formula. Usually this will be the first letter of the word which describes the variable. For example, V often represents volume and A is often used for area.

Example 10.10   Find an expression for the sum, S, of any three consecutive whole numbers.

Let the smallest number be n.

The next number is $(n + 1)$ and the third number is $(n + 2)$. So,

$$S = n + (n + 1) + (n + 2)$$
$$S = n + n + 1 + n + 2$$
$$S = 3n + 3$$

Example 10.11 ▷ How many months are there in   **i** 5 years

                                                   ii t years?

There are 12 months in a year, so   **i** in 5 years there will be $12 \times 5 = 60$ months

                                                   ii in t years there will be $12 \times t = 12t$ months

Exercise 10F

1 Using the letters suggested, construct a simple formula in each case.

  a The sum, S, of three numbers a, b and c.

  b The product, P, of two numbers x and y.

  c The difference, D, between the ages of two people. The older person is a years old and the other is b years old.

  d The sum, S, of four consecutive integers.

  e The number of days, D, in W weeks.

  f The average age, A, of three boys whose ages are m, n and p years.

2 How many days are there in:

  a 1 week   **b** 3 weeks   **c** w weeks?

3 A girl is now 13 years old.

  a How many years old will she be in:

      i 1 year   **ii** 5 years   **iii** t years?

  b How many years old was she:

      i 1 year ago   **ii** 3 years ago   **ii** m years ago?

4 A car travels at a speed of 30 mph. How many miles will it travel in:

  a 1 hour   **b** 2 hours   **c** t hours?

5 How many grams are there in:

  a 1 kg   **b** 5 kg   **c** x kg?

6 How many minutes are there in m hours?

7 Write down the number that is half as big as:

  a 20   **b** 6   **c** b

8 Write down the number that is twice as big as:

  a 4   **b** 7   **c** T

9 If a boy runs at b miles per hour, how many miles does he run in k hours?

10 **a** What is the cost, in pence, of 6 papers at 35 pence each?

     b What is the cost, in pence, of k papers at 35 pence each?

     c What is the cost, in pence, of k papers at q pence each?

11 A boy is b years old and his mother is 6 times as old.

    a   Find the mother's age in terms of b.

    b   Find the sum of their ages in y years time.

12 Mr Speed's age is equal to the sum of the ages of his three sons. The youngest son is aged x years, the eldest is 10 years older than the youngest and the middle son is 4 years younger than the eldest. How old is Mr Speed?

Extension Work

1   A man is now three times as old as his daughter. In 10 years time, the sum of their ages will be 76 years. How old was the man when his daughter was born?

2   Find three consecutive odd numbers for which the sum is 57.

3   A group of students had to choose between playing football and badminton. The number of students who chose football was three times the number who chose badminton. The number of players for each game would be equal if 12 students who chose football were asked to play badminton. Find the total number of students.

What you need to know for level 4

- How to solve simple linear equations
- Be able to substitute whole numbers into an expression

What you need to know for level 5

- How to construct expressions and formulae
- How to use simple formulae

National Curriculum SATs questions

LEVEL 5

1 *2002 Paper 1*

Look at this table:

	Age in years
Ann	a
Ben	b
Cindy	c

Copy the table below and write in words the meaning of each equation.
The first one is done for you.

a	$b = 30$	Ben is 30 years old
b	$a + b = 69$	
c	$b = 2c$	
d	$\frac{a + b + c}{3} = 28$	

2 **a** Copy the expressions below and work out their values when $x = 5$.

i $2x + 13$

ii $5x - 5$

iii $3 + 6x$

b When $2y + 11 = 17$, work out the value of y. Show your working.

3 You can often use algebra to show why a number puzzle works. Copy the right-hand column of the diagram below and fill in the missing expressions.

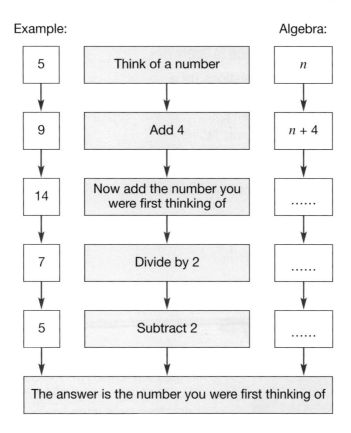

Example: Algebra:

5	Think of a number	n
9	Add 4	$n + 4$
14	Now add the number you were first thinking of	......
7	Divide by 2	......
5	Subtract 2	......

The answer is the number you were first thinking of

Handling Data **2**

This chapter is going to show you

- how to write questions for a questionnaire
- how to collect data
- how to use two-way tables
- how to construct statistical diagrams for discrete data
- how to construct stem and leaf diagrams

What you should already know

- How to interpret data from tables, graphs and charts
- How to find mode, median, mean and range for small data sets
- How to write a short report of a statistical survey
- How to design a data-collection sheet

Statistical surveys

In the picture the two teenagers are carrying out a survey about healthy eating. Do you think that their results will be fair if they only interview people who are buying burgers? How can they collect the data and make sure that many different opinions are obtained? How many people do you think they should ask?

Example 11.1

Here are some questions that might be used in a survey. Give a reason why each question is not very good. Then write a better question.

- **a** How old are you?   **b** Do you eat lots of fruit or vegetables?
- **c** Don't you agree that exercise is good for you?
- **d** If you go to a sports centre with your friends and you want to play badminton, do you usually play a doubles match or do you just practise?

- **a** This is a personal question. If you want to find out the ages of people, use answer boxes and put the ages in groups.

  How old are you?
  ☐ 0–15   ☐ 16–30   ☐ 31–45   ☐ 46–50   ☐ More than 50

- **b** This question is asking about two different items, so the answers may be confusing. It may be awkward to answer 'Yes' or 'No'. It is better to have several separate questions, such as:

  Do you eat fruit?   Do you eat vegetables?   How many portions do you eat?

- **c** This question is trying to force the people interviewed to agree. It is a leading question. A better question would be:

  Is exercise good for you?

- **d** This question is too long. There is too much information, which makes it difficult to understand. Replace with several shorter questions.

Choose one of the statements given below for your statistical survey, or make up your own and get your teacher to check it. For the statement you choose:

- Write down three or four questions for your questionnaire, which will test whether the statement is true.
- Decide how you will record your data.
- Make a data-collection sheet.
- Collect information from at least 30 people/observations.

1 Girls spend more on clothes than boys.

2 Old people use libraries more than teenagers.

3 When people holiday abroad one year, they tend to stay in Britain the following year.

4 Students who enjoy playing sports eat healthier foods.

5 Sports teams tend to score more towards the end of matches, as the opponents become tired.

7 Taller people have longer hair.

8 More men wear glasses than women.

9 Families eat out more than they used to.

Extension Work

Take each problem statement from the exercise and write down how you would collect the data required. For example, would you collect the data using a questionnaire or by carrying out an experiment? Or would you collect the data from books, computer software or the Internet? Also, write a short report on, or make a list of the advantages and disadvantages, of each method.

Stem-and-leaf diagrams

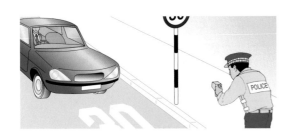

The speeds of vehicles in a 30 miles per-hour zone are recorded. The speeds are sorted into order and put into a stem-and-leaf diagram. The slowest speed is 23 miles per hour. The fastest speed is 45 miles per hour. How can you tell this from the stem-and-leaf diagram?

```
2 | 3  7  7  8  9  9
3 | 1  2  3  5  5  5  7  9
4 | 2  2  5
```

Key: 2 | 3 means 23 miles per hour

How many cars are breaking the speed limit?

Example 11.2 〉 A teacher asked 25 students how many pieces of homework they were given in one week. The results are shown in the stem-and-leaf diagram:

```
0 | 1  1  2  2  2  2  3  5  7  7  7  8  9
1 | 0  0  1  1  1  2  4  4  5  6
2 | 1  3                          Key: 1 | 2 means 12 homeworks
```

Use the stem-and-leaf diagram to find each of these:

a range   **b** mode

a The biggest number of homeworks is the last value, 23. The smallest number of homeworks is the first value, 1.

Range = Biggest value – Smallest value
= 23 – 1
= 22 homeworks

b The mode is the value which occurs the most. So, the mode = 2 homeworks because it occurs 4 times.

Exercise 11B

1 Fifteen sales people have a competition to find out who sells the most items in one day. Here are the results:

```
1 | 2  2  3  7  7
2 | 1  4  4  4  5  5  6
3 | 0  2  5                Key: 1 | 2 means 12 items
```

a How many items did the winner sell?   **b** What is the mode?
c Find the range.

2 35 Year 8 students are asked to estimate how many text messages they send on their mobile phones each week. Their replies are put into a stem-and-leaf diagram.

```
0 | 5  5  6  7  8  8
1 | 0  0  0  0  0  1  1  4  4
1 | 8  9  9  9
2 | 0  0  1  3  3  3  4
2 | 5  6
3 | 0  0  4
3 | 5  6  6              Key: 0 | 5 means 5 text messages
```

Work out each of the following:
a mode   **b** smallest estimate   **c** range

3 A farmer records the number of animals of each type on his farm. His results are shown in the stem-and-leaf diagram:

```
5 | 2  6  8
6 | 5  9
7 | 5              Key: 5 | 2 represents 52 animals of one type
```

a He has more sheep than any other type of animal. How many sheep does he have?
b How many animals has he altogether?

130

4 The ages of 30 people at a disco are shown on the right.

32	12	47	25	23	23	17	36	42	17
31	15	24	49	19	31	23	34	36	45
47	12	39	11	26	23	22	38	48	17

a Put the ages into a stem-and-leaf diagram. (Remember to show the key.)

b State the mode.

c Work out the range.

Extension Work

Look again at Example 11.2. The results are:

```
0 | 1  1  2  2  2  2  3  5  7  7  7  8  9
1 | 0  0  1  1  1  2  4  4  5  6
2 | 1  3                          Key: 1 | 2 means 12 homeworks
```

The **median** of a set of data is the middle value. Because there are 25 pupils, the middle value is the 13th, so the median is 9.

Now go back to Exercise 11B and see whether you can work out the median for Questions 1 and 2.

Pie charts

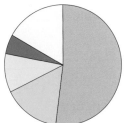

In the picture, which colour represents 'Unfit adults'? How do you know?

The pie chart is used because it shows the proportion of the whole amount and is quite easy to interpret.

Sometimes you will have to read information from pie charts, and sometimes you will be asked to draw them.

Example 11.3 ▷ The table shows how a group of people travel to work. Draw a pie chart to show the data. Label it clearly.

Type of travel	Walk	Car	Bus	Train
Frequency	4	16	12	8

The data adds up to 40 people. So, each sector on the ten-sector pie chart represents 4 people.

So, Walk gets 1 sector, Car gets 4 sectors (as 4 × 4 = 16), Bus gets 3 sectors (as 3 × 4 = 12), and Train gets 2 sectors (as 2 × 4 = 8).

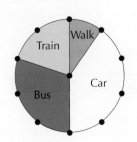

Example 11.4 ▷ The table on the right shows the favourite drinks of a group of Year 8 students.

Drink	% of students
Cola	40
Orange	25
Water	30
Coffee	5

Each sector on the ten-sector pie charts represents 10%.

So, Cola (40%) gets 4 sectors, Orange (25%) gets $2\frac{1}{2}$, Water (30%) gets 3 sectors, and Coffee (5%) gets $\frac{1}{2}$ sector.

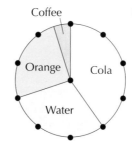

Exercise 11C

1 Draw pie charts to represent the following data.

a The favourite subject of 30 students:

Subject	Maths	English	Science	Languages
Number of students	12	6	8	4

b The types of food that 40 people usually eat for breakfast:

Food	Cereal	Toast	Fruit	Cooked	None
Number of people	12	8	6	10	4

c The number of goals scored by an ice-hockey team in 20 matches:

Goals	0	1	2	3	4
Number of matches	2	4	6	5	3

d The favourite colour of 60 Year 8 students:

Colour	Red	Green	Blue	Other
Number of students	18	6	24	12

2 The pie chart shows the results of a survey of 50 children about their favourite foods.

How many chose each of these?

a Chips **b** Burgers
c Fish fingers **d** Curry

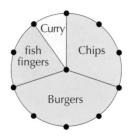

Design a poster to show information about 20 students in your class. Either include pie charts that you have drawn yourself or use a spreadsheet to produce the pie charts. Make sure that any pie chart you produce has labels and is easy to understand.

Scatter graphs

A doctor records the size of the pupils of people's eyes and the brightness of the sunlight. He then plots the results on a graph. What can you tell about the connection between the brightness and the pupil size of this group of people?

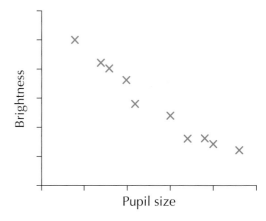

Example 11.5 Below are three scatter graphs. Describe the relationships in each graph.

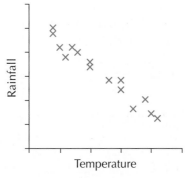

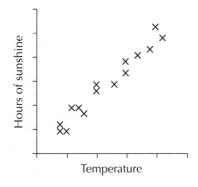

The first graph shows **negative correlation**. Here, this means that the higher the temperature, the less rainfall there is. That is, as one quantity increases, the other quantity decreases.

The second graph shows **positive correlation**. Here, this means that the higher the temperature, the more hours of sunshine there are. That is, as one quantity increases, so does the other quantity.

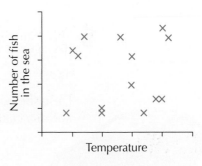

The third graph shows **no correlation**. Here, this means that there is no connection between the temperature and the number of fish in the sea.

1 **a** Describe the relationship between the price of tickets and the number of tickets sold.

b Describe the relationship between the midday temperature and the number of seaside visitors.

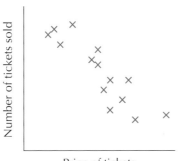

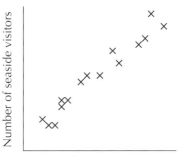

2 A survey is carried out to compare students' ages with the amount of money that they spend each week. The data is shown on the scatter diagram.

Describe what the graph tells you.

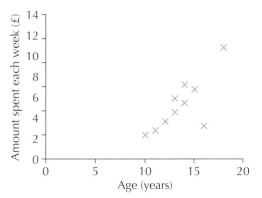

3 A survey was carried out to compare how much time per week students spend watching television with how much time they spend on homework. The data is shown on the scatter graph.

Describe what the graph tells you.

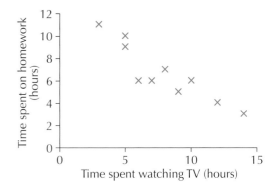

4 The scatter graph shows the values of a make of car plotted against its age.

Describe what the graph tells you about a car's value as it gets older.

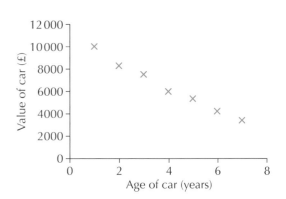

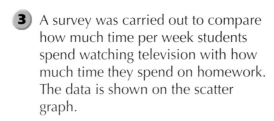

5 The table shows the average number of hours sleep that a sample of people of different ages have.

Age	10	15	20	25	30	35	40	45	50	60
Amount of sleep (hours)	9	8.5	7	7	6.5	7	6	6	5	4.5

a Copy the scatter graph axes and plot the points. The first two points have been done for you.

b Describe what the graph tells you about the relationship between age and amount of sleep.

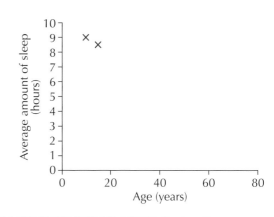

Extension Work

Put two columns in your exercise book. Write down pairs of events that have negative, positive or no correlation. In each case, indicate the type of correlation.

Analysing data

Suppose that you want to put some data into the form of diagrams or tables. How do you choose which form to use? Ask yourself a few questions. Will my diagram be easy to understand? If I use a pie chart, will there be too many sectors? Am I comparing two sets of data?

Once you have collected your data, you should write a report which contains:

- A sentence saying what you think the data will tell you.
- A bar chart and one or two facts that you have found out from the bar chart.
- A pie chart and at least one additional fact that you have found out from the pie chart.
- A sentence about the piece of data which appears most often (the mode).
- A stem and leaf diagram or scatter graph and any other diagrams that that you consider useful.

- The analysis of your data could take the form of:
  - Calculations to find the mode and range.
  - One or two sentences about what the diagrams and graphs tell you.
  - Other graphs produced using ICT software (but make sure that you understand them).
- When analysing your data try to explain why you have chosen to draw each type of diagram.
- Write a brief conclusion which refers back to your first sentence. Comment on any other features that you can see from your graphs and diagrams.

Exercise **11E**

For each statement/question below, write down which of these methods is the best way to collect data:

- Survey
- Questionnaire
- Controlled experiment
- Data from textbooks or the Internet

1 More men attend sports events than women.

2 It always snows in December.

3 Is a dice you are given fair?

4 Which soap powder is most popular?

5 What percentage of 13-year-old children have mobile phones?

6 How popular is a particular restaurant?

7 How many people have had an illness in the past 2 months?

8 Do Year 8 girls prefer to watch Brad Pitt or Tom Cruise?

9 How many people visit a shopping centre on a Sunday?

10 How many lorries use a road between 8.00 am and 9.00 am?

Extension Work

Write your report, including as much detail as possible, using the guidelines given in this chapter.

You can use the data given below about a survey of the newspapers that people read or your own data from Exercise 11A.

| Newspaper | Number of readers | |
	Male	Female
Echo	38	23
Herald	10	53
Chronicle	50	12
Recorder	35	45
Gazette	32	20
Examiner	15	27
Total	**180**	**180**

National Curriculum SATs questions

LEVEL 4

1 *1997 Paper 2*

There are 50 children altogether in a playgroup.

a How many of the children are girls?
What percentage of the children are girls?

b 25 of the children are 4 years old.
20 of the children are 3 years old.
5 of the children are 2 years old.

Show this information on a copy of the diagram on the right.

Label each part clearly.

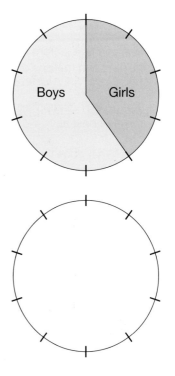

LEVEL 5

2 *2001 Paper 1*

There are 60 pupils in a school. 6 of these pupils wear glasses.

a The pie chart is not drawn accurately.

What should the angles be? Show your working.

b Exactly half of the 60 pupils in the school are boys.

From this information, is the percentage of boys in this
school that wear glasses 5%, 6%, 10%, 20%, 50% or not possible to tell?

3 *2001 Paper 2*

A teacher asked two different classes: 'What type of book is your favourite?'

a Results from Class A (total 20 pupils) are shown on the right.

Draw a pie chart to show this information. Show your working and draw your angles accurately.

Type of book	Frequency
Crime	3
Non-fiction	13
Fantasy	4

b The pie chart on the right shows the results from all of Class B.

Each pupil had only one vote.

The sector for non-fiction represents 11 pupils.

How many pupils are in Class B? Show your working.

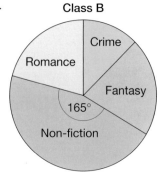

Class B

4 *1999 Paper 1*

The scatter diagram shows the heights and masses of some horses.

The scatter diagram also shows a line of best fit.

a What does the scatter diagram show about the relationship between the height and mass of horses?

b The height of a horse is 163 cm.

Use the line of best fit to estimate the mass of the horse (in kg).

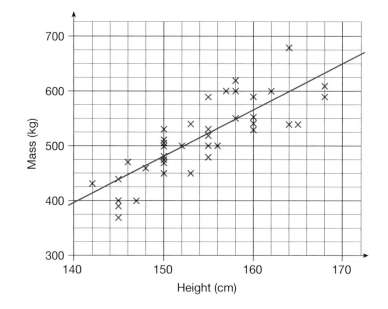

c A different horse has a mass of 625 kg.

Use the line of best fit to estimate the height of the horse (in cm).

d A teacher asks his class to investigate this statement:

'The length of the back leg of a horse is always less than the length of the front leg of a horse.'

What might a scatter graph look like if the statement is correct? Take the *x*-axis as the length of the front leg from 70 to 110 cm. Take the *y*-axis to be the length of the back leg from 70 to 110 cm.

5 *1998 Paper 2*

A competition has three different games.

a Jeff plays two games. To win, Jeff needs a mean score of 60.

How many points does he need to score in Game C? Show your working.

	Game A	Game B	Game C
Score	62	53	

b Imran and Nia play the three games. Their scores have the same mean.

The range of Imran's scores is twice the range of Nia's scores. Copy the table above and fill in the missing scores.

Imran's scores		40	
Nia's scores	35	40	45

The scatter diagrams show the scores of everyone who plays all three games.

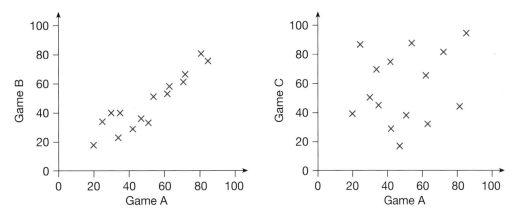

c Look at the scatter diagrams.

Which statement most closely describes the relationship between the games?

Game A and Game B				
Perfect negative	Negative	No relationship	Positive	Perfect positive

Game A and Game C				
Perfect negative	Negative	No relationship	Positive	Perfect positive

d What can you tell about the relationship between the scores on Game B and the scores on Game C?

Game B and Game C				
Perfect negative	Negative	No relationship	Positive	Perfect positive

This chapter is going to show you	**What you should already know**
○ how to add and subtract fractions with any denominators ○ how to use BODMAS with more complex problems ○ how to solve problems using decimals, fractions, percentages and units of measurement	○ How to add and subtract fractions with the same denominator ○ How to find equivalent fractions ○ How to use the four operations with decimals

Fractions

This section recalls some of the rules you have already met about fractions.

Example 12.1   Work out:

a   How many sevenths are in 4 whole ones.

b   How many fifths are in $3\frac{3}{5}$.

a   There are 7 sevenths in one whole, so there are $4 \times 7 = 28$ sevenths in 4 whole ones.

b   There are $3 \times 5 = 15$ fifths in 3 whole ones, so there are $15 + 3 = 18$ fifths in $3\frac{3}{5}$.

Example 12.2   Write the following as mixed numbers:

a $\frac{48}{15}$ **b** $\frac{24}{18}$

a $48 \div 15 = 3$ remainder 3, so $\frac{48}{15} = 3\frac{3}{15}$, which can cancel to $3\frac{1}{5}$.

Note it is usually easier to cancel after the fraction has been written as a mixed number rather than before.

b $24 \div 18 = 1$ remainder 6, so $\frac{24}{18} = 1\frac{6}{18}$, which is $1\frac{1}{3}$ in its simplest form.

Exercise 12A   **1** Find the missing number in each of these fractions:

a $\frac{5}{3} = \frac{\square}{9}$ **b** $\frac{9}{8} = \frac{\square}{16}$ **c** $\frac{25}{9} = \frac{\square}{27}$

d $\frac{8}{5} = \frac{\square}{15}$ **e** $\frac{12}{7} = \frac{48}{\square}$ **f** $\frac{20}{9} = \frac{80}{\square}$

g $\frac{8}{5} = \frac{\square}{15}$ **h** $\frac{7}{2} = \frac{\square}{6}$ **i** $\frac{13}{3} = \frac{52}{\square}$

2 **a** How many sixths are in $3\frac{5}{6}$? **b** How many eighths are in $4\frac{1}{2}$?

c How many tenths are in $2\frac{2}{5}$? **d** How many ninths are in $5\frac{7}{9}$?

3 Convert each of these top-heavy fractions to a mixed number:

a $\frac{3}{2}$ **b** $\frac{7}{5}$ **c** $\frac{9}{7}$ **d** $\frac{17}{8}$ **e** $\frac{15}{2}$ **f** $\frac{22}{7}$

g $\frac{32}{15}$ **h** $\frac{17}{5}$ **i** $\frac{12}{5}$ **j** $\frac{13}{6}$ **k** $\frac{9}{4}$ **l** $\frac{41}{10}$

4 Convert each of these mixed numbers to a top-heavy fraction:

a $1\frac{1}{4}$ **b** $2\frac{1}{2}$ **c** $3\frac{1}{6}$ **d** $4\frac{2}{7}$ **e** $5\frac{1}{8}$ **f** $2\frac{3}{5}$

g $1\frac{7}{8}$ **h** $3\frac{3}{4}$ **i** $3\frac{2}{5}$ **j** $2\frac{3}{11}$ **k** $4\frac{5}{8}$ **l** $3\frac{2}{9}$

5 Write each of the following as a mixed number in its simplest form:

a $\frac{14}{12}$ **b** $\frac{15}{9}$ **c** $\frac{24}{21}$ **d** $\frac{35}{20}$

e $\frac{28}{20}$ **f** $\frac{70}{50}$ **g** $\frac{28}{24}$ **h** $\frac{26}{12}$

i $\frac{44}{24}$ **j** $\frac{32}{10}$ **k** $\frac{36}{24}$ **l** $\frac{75}{35}$

6 Write these fractions as mixed numbers (cancel down if necessary):

a seven thirds **b** sixteen sevenths **c** twelve fifths **d** nine halves

e $\frac{20}{7}$ **f** $\frac{24}{5}$ **g** $\frac{13}{3}$ **h** $\frac{19}{8}$ **i** $\frac{146}{12}$ **j** $\frac{78}{10}$ **k** $\frac{52}{12}$ **l** $\frac{102}{9}$

Extension Work

Write as fractions:

a the fraction of a metre given by:

i 715 cm **ii** 2300 mm **iii** 405 cm

iv 580 cm **v** 1550 mm **vi** 225 cm

b the fraction of a kilogram given by:

i 2300 g **ii** 4050 g **iii** 7500 g

iv 5600 g **v** 1225 g **vi** 6580 g

Adding and subtracting fractions

When the denominators of two fractions are not the same, they must be made the same before the numerators are added or subtracted. To do this, we need to find the Lowest Common Multiple (LCM) of the denominators.

Example 12.3 Add together:

a $\frac{2}{5}+\frac{1}{4}$ **b** $\frac{2}{3}+\frac{2}{7}$ **c** $\frac{1}{3}+\frac{5}{6}+\frac{3}{4}$

a The common denominator is 20, as this is the lowest common multiple of 20, hence $\frac{2}{5}+\frac{1}{4}=\frac{8}{20}+\frac{5}{20}=\frac{13}{20}$

b The common denominator is 21, so $\frac{2}{3}+\frac{2}{7}=\frac{14}{21}+\frac{6}{21}=\frac{20}{21}$

c The common denominator is 12, so $\frac{1}{3}+\frac{5}{6}+\frac{3}{4}=\frac{4}{12}+\frac{10}{12}+\frac{9}{12}=\frac{23}{12}=1\frac{11}{12}$

Note that the last answer is a top-heavy fraction, so should be written as a mixed number.

Example 12.4 ▷ Subtract:

a $\frac{2}{3} - \frac{1}{4}$ **b** $\frac{5}{6} - \frac{4}{9}$

a Common denominator is 12, so $\frac{2}{3} - \frac{1}{4} = \frac{8}{12} - \frac{3}{12} = \frac{5}{12}$

b Common denominator is 18, so $\frac{5}{6} - \frac{4}{9} = \frac{15}{18} - \frac{8}{18} = \frac{7}{18}$

Exercise 12B

1 Find the lowest common multiple of the following pairs of numbers:

a (3, 4)   **b** (5, 6)   **c** (3, 5)   **d** (2, 3)

e (4, 5)   **f** (2, 4)   **g** (6, 9)   **h** (4, 6)

2 Add the following fractions:

a $\frac{2}{3} + \frac{1}{4}$ **b** $\frac{2}{5} + \frac{1}{6}$ **c** $\frac{1}{3} + \frac{2}{5}$ **d** $\frac{1}{3} + \frac{1}{2}$

e $\frac{1}{5} + \frac{1}{4}$ **f** $\frac{1}{2} + \frac{1}{4}$ **g** $\frac{5}{6} + \frac{1}{9}$ **h** $\frac{1}{6} + \frac{1}{4}$

3 Subtract the following fractions:

a $\frac{1}{3} - \frac{1}{4}$ **b** $\frac{2}{5} - \frac{1}{6}$ **c** $\frac{2}{5} - \frac{1}{3}$ **d** $\frac{1}{2} - \frac{1}{3}$

e $\frac{2}{5} - \frac{1}{4}$ **f** $\frac{1}{2} - \frac{1}{4}$ **g** $\frac{5}{6} - \frac{1}{9}$ **h** $\frac{5}{6} - \frac{3}{4}$

4 Convert the following fractions to equivalent fractions with a common denominator, and then work out the answer, cancelling down or writing as a mixed number if appropriate:

a $\frac{1}{3} + \frac{1}{4}$ **b** $\frac{1}{6} + \frac{1}{3}$ **c** $\frac{3}{10} + \frac{1}{4}$ **d** $\frac{1}{8} + \frac{5}{6}$

e $\frac{4}{15} + \frac{3}{10}$ **f** $\frac{7}{8} + \frac{5}{6}$ **g** $\frac{7}{12} + \frac{1}{4}$ **h** $\frac{3}{4} + \frac{1}{3} + \frac{1}{2}$

i $\frac{2}{3} - \frac{1}{8}$ **j** $\frac{5}{6} - \frac{1}{3}$ **k** $\frac{3}{10} - \frac{1}{4}$ **l** $\frac{8}{9} - \frac{1}{6}$

m $\frac{4}{15} - \frac{1}{10}$ **n** $\frac{7}{8} - \frac{5}{6}$ **o** $\frac{7}{12} - \frac{1}{4}$ **p** $\frac{3}{4} + \frac{1}{3} - \frac{1}{2}$

Extension Work

The ancient Egyptians only used unit fractions, that is fractions with a numerator of 1. So they would write $\frac{5}{8}$ as $\frac{1}{2} + \frac{1}{8}$.

1 Write the following as the sum of two unit fractions:

a $\frac{3}{8}$ **b** $\frac{3}{4}$

c $\frac{7}{12}$ **d** $\frac{2}{3}$

2 Write the following as the sum of three unit fractions:

a $\frac{7}{8}$ **b** $\frac{5}{6}$

c $\frac{5}{8}$ **d** $\frac{23}{24}$

BODMAS

You have met BODMAS in Year 7. It gives the order in which mathematical operations are carried out.

Remember that if we have a calculation that is a string of additions and subtractions, or a string of multiplications and divisions, then we do the calculation from left to right.

B	– Brackets
O	– pOwers
DM	– Division and Multiplication
AS	– Addition and Subtraction

Example 12.5 ▷ Work out each of the following, using the order of operations given by BODMAS. Show each step of the calculation.

a $10 - 3 \times 2$ **b** $5 \times (7 + 3) - 5$ **c** $18 \div 3 \times 2$

a Firstly, work out the multiplication, which gives $10 - 6$
Then work out the subtraction to give 4

b Firstly, work out the bracket, which gives $5 \times 10 - 5$
Secondly, the multiplication, which gives $50 - 5$
Finally, the subtraction to give 45

c There is a choice between division and multiplication, so decide on the order by working from left to right:
Work out the left-hand operation first, which gives 6×2
Then work out the remaining operation to give 12

Example 12.6 ▷ Work out:

a $2 \times 3^2 + 6 \div 2$ **b** $(2 + 3)^2 \times 8 - 6$

Show each step of the calculation.

a Firstly, work out the power, which gives $2 \times 9 + 6 \div 2$
Secondly, the division and multiplication, which gives $18 + 3$
Finally, the addition to give 21

b Firstly, work out the bracket, which gives $5^2 \times 8 - 6$
Secondly, the power, which gives $25 \times 8 - 6$
Thirdly, the multiplication, which gives $200 - 6$
Finally, the subtraction to give 194

Exercise 12C

1 Write the operation that you do first in each of these calculations, and then work out each calculation:

a $5 + 4 \times 7$ **b** $18 - 6 \div 3$ **c** $7 \times 7 + 2$ **d** $16 \div 4 - 2$

e $(5 + 4) \times 7$ **f** $(18 - 6) \div 3$ **g** $7 \times (7 + 2)$ **h** $16 \div (4 - 2)$

i $5 + 9 - 7 - 2$ **j** $2 \times 6 \div 3 \times 4$ **k** $12 - 15 + 7$ **l** $12 \div 3 \times 6 \div 2$

2 Work out the following, showing each step of the calculation:

a $3 + 4 + 4^2$ b $3 + (4 + 4)^2$ c $3 \times 4 + 4^2$ d $3 \times (4 + 4)^2$

e $5 + 3^2 - 7$ f $(5 + 3)^2 - 7$ g $2 \times 6^2 + 2$ h $2 \times (6^2 + 2)$

i $\dfrac{200}{4 \times 5}$ j $\dfrac{80 + 20}{4 \times 5}$ k $\sqrt{(4^2 + 3^2)}$ l $\dfrac{(2 + 3)^2}{6 - 1}$

m $3.2 - (5.4 + 6.1) + (5.7 - 2.1)$ n $8 \times (12 \div 4) \div (2 \times 2)$

3 Write out each of the following and insert brackets to make the calculation true:

a $3 \times 7 + 1 = 24$ b $3 + 7 \times 2 = 20$ c $2 \times 3 + 1 \times 4 = 32$

d $2 + 3^2 = 25$ e $5 \times 5 + 5 \div 5 = 26$ f $5 \times 5 + 5 \div 5 = 10$

g $5 \times 5 + 5 \div 5 = 6$ h $15 - 3^2 = 144$

Extension Work

By putting brackets in different places, one calculation can be made to give many different answers. For example:

$$4 \times 6 + 4 - 3 \times 8 + 1 = 24 + 4 - 24 + 1 = 5$$

without brackets, but with brackets, it could be:

$$4 \times (6 + 4) - 3 \times (8 + 1) = 4 \times 10 - 3 \times 9 = 40 - 27 = 13$$

By putting brackets into the appropriate places in the calculation above, obtain answers of:

a 33   b 17   c 252   d 1

Multiplying decimals

This section will give you more practice on multiplying integers and decimals.

Example 12.7   Find:

a 0.2×0.3 b 40×0.8

a $2 \times 3 = 6$. There are two decimal places in the multiplication, so there are two in the answer. So, $0.2 \times 0.3 = 0.06$.

b Rewrite the problem as an equivalent product, that is $40 \times 0.8 = 4 \times 8 = 32$

Example 12.8   A sheet of card is 0.5 mm thick. How thick is a pack of card containing 80 sheets?

This is a multiplication problem:

$0.5 \times 80 = 5 \times 8 = 40$ mm

1 Without using a calculator, write down the answers to:

a	0.2×0.3	**b**	0.4×0.2	**c**	0.6×0.6	**d**	0.7×0.2
e	0.2×0.4	**f**	0.8×0.4	**g**	0.6×0.1	**h**	0.3×0.3
i	0.7×0.8	**j**	0.5×0.8	**k**	0.9×0.3	**l**	0.6×0.9

2 Without using a calculator, work out:

a	30×0.8	**b**	0.6×20	**c**	0.6×50	**d**	0.2×60
e	0.3×40	**f**	0.4×50	**g**	0.7×20	**h**	0.2×90
i	0.5×80	**j**	70×0.6	**k**	30×0.1	**l**	80×0.6

3 Without using a calculator, work out:

a	0.02×0.4	**b**	0.8×0.04	**c**	0.07×0.08	**d**	0.006×0.9
e	0.8×0.005	**f**	0.06×0.03	**g**	0.01×0.02	**h**	0.07×0.07

4 Without using a calculator, work out:

a	300×0.8	**b**	0.06×400	**c**	0.6×500	**d**	0.02×600
e	0.005×8000	**f**	300×0.01	**g**	600×0.006	**h**	0.04×8000

4 Screws cost 0.6p. A company orders 2000 screws. How much will this cost?

5 A grain of sand weighs 0.6 milligrams. How much would 500 grains weigh?

Extension Work

This extension work is about using powers with decimals.
$$0.1 \times 0.1 = 0.1^2 = 0.01$$
$$0.1 \times 0.1 \times 0.1 = 0.1^3 = 0.001$$
$$0.1 \times 0.1 \times 0.1 \times 0.1 = 0.1^4 = 0.0001$$

Using the calculations above, write down the answers to:

a	0.1^5	**b**	0.1^6	**c**	0.1^7	**d**	0.1^{10}

Write down the answers to:

e	0.2^2	**f**	0.3^2	**g**	0.4^2	**h**	0.5^2
i	0.2^3	**j**	0.3^3	**k**	0.4^3	**l**	0.5^3

Dividing decimals

This section gives more practice on dividing integers and decimals.

Example 12.9 Work out:

    a $0.8 \div 0.2$ **b** $20 \div 0.5$ **c** $0.16 \div 0.4$ **d** $400 \div 0.8$

    a Rewrite the sum as equivalent divisions, $0.8 \div 0.2 = 8 \div 2 = 4$. You must multiply both numbers by 10 at a time, to keep the calculation equivalent.

    b Rewriting this as equivalent divisions gives:
$$20 \div 0.5 = 200 \div 5 = 40$$

    c Rewriting this as equivalent divisions gives:
$$0.16 \div 0.4 = 1.6 \div 4 = 0.4$$

    d Rewriting this as equivalent divisions gives:
$$400 \div 0.8 = 4000 \div 8 = 500$$

Exercise 12E

1 Without using a calculator, work out:

a $0.4 \div 0.2$	**b** $0.6 \div 0.2$	**c** $0.6 \div 0.1$	**d** $0.9 \div 0.3$
e $0.2 \div 0.1$	**f** $0.8 \div 0.2$	**g** $0.18 \div 0.3$	**h** $0.12 \div 0.3$
i $0.16 \div 0.2$	**j** $0.8 \div 0.2$	**k** $0.8 \div 0.1$	**l** $0.24 \div 0.8$
m $0.2 \div 0.2$	**n** $0.8 \div 0.8$	**o** $0.9 \div 0.9$	**p** $0.4 \div 0.1$

2 Without using a calculator, work out:

a $200 \div 0.4$	**b** $300 \div 0.2$	**c** $40 \div 0.8$	**d** $200 \div 0.2$
e $90 \div 0.3$	**f** $40 \div 0.4$	**g** $50 \div 0.1$	**h** $400 \div 0.2$
i $300 \div 0.5$	**j** $400 \div 0.5$	**k** $400 \div 0.1$	**l** $200 \div 0.1$
m $30 \div 0.5$	**n** $50 \div 0.5$	**o** $60 \div 0.5$	**p** $400 \div 0.4$

Example 12.10 Work out the calculations below. These contain more decimal places than those you have been doing.

    a $0.8 \div 0.04$ **b** $0.04 \div 0.2$ **c** $50 \div 0.02$

In each case, rewrite as an equivalent calculation, so that the division is by a whole-number.

    a $0.8 \div 0.04 = 8 \div 0.4 = 80 \div 4 = 20$

    b $0.04 \div 0.2 = 0.4 \div 2 = 0.2$

    c $50 \div 0.02 = 500 \div 0.2 = 5000 \div 2 = 2500$

3 Without using a calculator, work out:

a $0.4 \div 0.02$	**b** $0.06 \div 0.1$	**c** $0.9 \div 0.03$
d $0.2 \div 0.01$	**e** $0.06 \div 0.02$	**f** $0.09 \div 0.3$

4 Without using a calculator, work out:

a $40 \div 0.08$ b $200 \div 0.02$ c $400 \div 0.05$

d $200 \div 0.01$ e $24 \div 0.02$ f $4000 \div 0.02$

4 Bolts cost 0.3p. How many can I buy with £60 (= 6000p)?

5 Grains of salt weigh 0.2 mg. How many grains are in a kilogram (= 1 000 000 mg) of salt?

Extension Work

1 Given that $46 \times 34 = 1564$, write down the answers to:

a 4.6×34 b 4.6×3.4 c $1564 \div 3.4$ d $15.64 \div 0.034$

2 Given that $57 \times 32 = 1824$, write down the answers to:

a 5.7×0.032 b $0.57 \times 32\,000$ c 5700×0.32 d 0.0057×32

3 Given that $2.8 \times 0.55 = 1.540$, write down the answers to:

a 28×55 b $154 \div 55$ c $15.4 \div 0.028$ d 0.028×5500

What you need to know for level 4

○ How to work out equivalent fractions and mixed numbers
○ How to add and subtract fractions

What you need to know for level 5

○ How to manipulate fractions and mixed numbers
○ The order in which the four operations must be used
○ How to multiply and divide integers and decimals

National Curriculum SATs questions

LEVEL 4

1 *2000 Paper 1*

Mark and James have the same birthday. They were born on 15th March in different years.

a Mark will be 12 years old on 15 March 2001.

How old will he be on 15 March 2010?

b In which year was Mark born?

c James was half of Mark's age on 15 March 2001. In what year was James born?

2 *2001 Paper 2*

Look at this number chain.

a Write down the missing numbers from the circles below.

b Write down the missing numbers from the arrows below.

LEVEL 5

3 *2001 Paper 2*

Some people use yards to measure length. The diagram shows one way to change yards to metres.

a Change 100 yards to metres.

b Change 100 metres to yards.

CHAPTER 13 Algebra 5

This chapter is going to show you

- how to expand and then simplify expressions
- how to solve a range of linear equations
- how to construct equations and solve them
- how to change the subject of a formula

What you should already know

- The arithmetic of negative numbers

Expansion of brackets

In algebra, brackets occur often. They may form part of all kinds of expressions and equations – from the simplest to the most complicated.

Expansion means removing the brackets from an expression or equation by multiplying each term inside the brackets by the term outside the brackets. Look at Example 13.1 to see how this works with numbers.

Example 13.1

Expand and simplify $3(5 + 2)$.

Multiply each term in the brackets by 3: $3 \times 5 + 3 \times 2$

$= 15 + 6 = 21$

Check by working out the bracket first: $3(5 + 2) = 3 \times 7 = 21$

The same rule can be applied to algebraic terms, as Example 13.2 shows.

Example 13.2

Expand each of these:

a $2(4 + 3y)$ **b** $3(5p - 2)$

a Multiply each term in the brackets by 2: $2(4 + 3y)$

$= 2 \times 4 + 2 \times 3y$

$= 8 + 6y$

b Multiply each term in the brackets by 3: $3(5p - 2)$

$= 3 \times 5p + 3 \times (-2)$

$= 15p + -6$

$= 15p - 6$

Note Neither $8 + 6y$ nor $15p - 6$ can be simplified because 8 and $6y$ are not like terms and neither are $15p$ and 6.

1 Copy and complete each of the following

   a $2(4 + 5)$ $= 2 \times 9 = \boxed{}$

       $2 \times 4 + 2 \times 5 = 8 + \boxed{} = \boxed{}$

       $2(4 + 5)$ $= 2 \times 4 + 2 \times 5$

   b $3(2 + 7)$ $= 3 \times \boxed{} = \boxed{}$

       $3 \times 2 + 3 \times 7 = \boxed{} + \boxed{} = \boxed{}$

       $3(2 + 7)$ $= \boxed{} \times \boxed{} + \boxed{} \times \boxed{}$

   c $5(4 + 3)$ $= \boxed{} \times \boxed{} = \boxed{}$

       $5 \times \boxed{} + 5 \times \boxed{} = \boxed{} + \boxed{} = \boxed{}$

       $5(4 + 3)$ $= \boxed{} \times \boxed{} + \boxed{} \times \boxed{}$

   d $4(5 + 2)$ $= \boxed{} \times \boxed{} = \boxed{}$

       $\boxed{} \times \boxed{} + \boxed{} \times \boxed{} = \boxed{} + \boxed{} = \boxed{}$

       $4(5 + 2)$ $= \boxed{} \times \boxed{} + \boxed{} \times \boxed{}$

2 Copy and complete each of the following.

   a $3(2 + t) = 3 \times 2 + 3 \times t = \boxed{} + \boxed{}$

   b $5(m + 4) = 5 \times m + 5 \times 4 = \boxed{} + \boxed{}$

   c $4(3 - k) = 4 \times 3 + 4 \times (-k) = \boxed{} - \boxed{}$

   d $2(w - 4) = 2 \times w + 2 \times (-4) = \boxed{} - \boxed{}$

   e $3(4 + k) = 3 \times \boxed{} + \boxed{} \times \boxed{} = \boxed{} + \boxed{}$

   f $5(q + 2) = \boxed{} \times \boxed{} + 5 \times \boxed{} = \boxed{} + \boxed{}$

   g $4(5 - t) = \boxed{} \times \boxed{} + \boxed{} \times \boxed{} = \boxed{} - \boxed{}$

   h $2(n - 3) = \boxed{} \times \boxed{} + \boxed{} \times \boxed{} = \boxed{} - \boxed{}$

3 Expand each of the following.

   a $3(4 + k)$ **b** $5(m + 7)$ **c** $4(3 + t)$ **d** $2(5 - n)$ **e** $3(w - 2)$

   f $6(h - 2)$ **g** $5(3 + g)$ **h** $2(f - 7)$ **i** $3(1 - q)$

4 Copy and complete each of the following.

   a $3(2m + 4) = 3 \times 2m + 3 \times 4 = 6m + \boxed{}$

   b $5(3 + 2t) = 5 \times 3 + 5 \times 2t = \boxed{} + \boxed{}$

   c $4(3w - 2) = 4 \times \boxed{} + 4 \times \boxed{} = \boxed{} - \boxed{}$

   d $2(5 + 4k) = 2 \times \boxed{} + 2 \times \boxed{} = \boxed{} + \boxed{}$

   e $3(5d + 2) = \boxed{} \times \boxed{} + \boxed{} \times \boxed{} = \boxed{} + \boxed{}$

   f $5(4 - 3q) = \boxed{} \times \boxed{} + \boxed{} \times \boxed{} = \boxed{} - \boxed{}$

   g $4(2n + 7) = \boxed{} \times \boxed{} + \boxed{} \times \boxed{} = \boxed{} + \boxed{}$

5 Expand each of the following.

a	$3(2a + 3)$	**b**	$2(4 - 3k)$	**c**	$5(1 + 3p)$
d	$4(2q - 3)$	**e**	$3(4 + 2t)$	**f**	$7(4 + 3m)$
g	$2(5y - 3)$	**h**	$4(3 - 2n)$	**i**	$5(2m + 4)$
j	$3(3p - 2)$	**k**	$6(5 + 3y)$	**l**	$2(3k - 4)$

Extension Work

In a magic square, each row, each column and each diagonal add up to the same amount.

1 Show that the square below is a magic square.

$x + m$	$x + y - m$	$x - y$
$x - y - m$	x	$x + y + m$
$x + y$	$x - y + m$	$x - m$

2 Using different values for x, y and m, see how many magic squares you can create.

Solving equations

You have met several different types of linear equation so far. They were solved by finding the inverse mapping of each equation.

Example 13.3

Solve each of these equations.

a $3x = 15$ **b** $n + 7 = 15$ **c** $4t - 3 = 17$

a $3x = 15$ gives:

$$x \longrightarrow \boxed{\times 3} \longrightarrow 15$$
$$5 \longleftarrow \boxed{\div 3} \longleftarrow 15$$

So, $x = 5$.

b $n + 7 = 15$ gives:

$$n \longrightarrow \boxed{+ 7} \longrightarrow 15$$
$$8 \longleftarrow \boxed{- 7} \longleftarrow 15$$

So, $n = 8$.

c $4t - 3 = 17$ gives:

$$t \longrightarrow \boxed{\times 4} \longrightarrow \boxed{- 3} \longrightarrow 17$$
$$5 \longleftarrow \boxed{\div 4} \longleftarrow \boxed{+ 3} \longleftarrow 17$$

So, $t = 5$.

When an equation has brackets in it, three operations are needed to solve the equation. Look at example 13.4 to see how this works.

Example 13.4 ▷ Solve $3(2x + 4) = 30$.

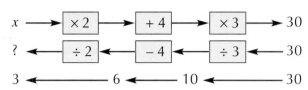

So, $x = 3$.

① Solve each of the following equations:

a $4x = 12$	**b** $5x = 30$	**c** $2m = 14$
d $3n = 15$	**e** $2x = 7$	**f** $2x = 11$
g $x + 7 = 8$	**h** $x + 3 = 18$	**i** $x + 5 = 23$
j $x - 3 = 11$	**k** $x - 4 = 17$	**l** $x + 3 = 19$

② Solve each of the following equations:

a $4n + 1 = 21$	**b** $5n + 3 = 18$	**c** $3m + 4 = 19$
d $7x + 2 = 23$	**e** $2x - 1 = 11$	**f** $4m - 3 = 17$
g $5x + 3 = 33$	**h** $2n - 7 = 15$	**i** $2k - 5 = 3$
j $10x + 7 = 47$	**k** $5x - 3 = 22$	**l** $4n + 17 = 25$

③ Solve each of the following equations:

a $3(2t + 5) = 33$	**b** $2(5m + 3) = 36$	**c** $5(2m + 1) = 45$
d $4(3k + 2) = 56$	**e** $2(2t - 3) = 18$	**f** $4(3x - 2) = 28$

④ Ewan's dad helped him with his homework, but he got most of it wrong. In each case, explain what is wrong and then correct it.

a $5x + 3 = 13$ $x = 13 - 5$ $x = 8$	**b** $3m - 4 = 11$ $m = 11 + 4 - 3$ $m = 12$
c $2(3x + 4) = 38$ $x = 38 \div 2 - 4 - 3$ $x = 12$	**d** $4(5m + 3) = 28$ $m = 28 \div 4 - 3 + 5$ $m = 9$

Extension Work

Solve each of the following equations.

a $1.5x + 3.6 = 5.4$	**b** $2.4x + 7.1 = 13.1$	**c** $3.4m - 4.3 = 7.6$
d $5.6k - 2.9 = 5.5$	**e** $4.5n - 3.7 = 12.5$	**f** $1.8t + 7.1 = 18.8$
g $28 - 3.6x = 11.8$	**h** $31.3 - 2.8x = 27.1$	**i** $2.4 - 1.8m = 8.7$

Constructing equations to solve

The first step in solving a problem using algebra is to write down an equation. This is called **constructing** an equation.

You need to choose a letter to stand for each variable in the problem. This might be x or the first letter of words which describe the variable. For example, t is often used to stand for time.

Example 13.6

I think of a number, multiply it by 5 and add 7 to the result. I get the answer 22. What is the number I first thought of?

Let my number be x.

Multiplying it by 5 gives: $5x$

Adding 7 to $5x$ gives: $5x + 7$

The answer has to be 22, so form the equation: $5x + 7 = 22$

Now solve the equation using inverse mapping:

$$5x + 7 = 22$$

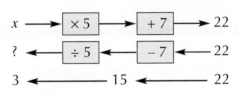

So my number is 3.

Exercise 13C

1 Write down an algebraic expression for each of the following.

a The number which is 5 more than x.

b The number which is 4 less than x.

c The number which is 17 more than m.

d The number which is 11 less than n.

e The number which is 3 times as large as q.

f The number which is twice the size of m.

2 a Two numbers add up to 100. If one of the numbers is x, write an expression for the other.

b The difference between two numbers is 8. If the smaller of the two numbers is y, write down an expression for the larger number.

c Jim and Ann have 18 marbles between them. If Jim has p marbles, how many marbles has Ann? Write an expression for this.

3 James thinks of a number rule.

Double the number and add 3.

a Using n for the number, write James's rule as an algebraic expression.

b James replies '17' when Helen gives him a number. Write down the equation this gives and solve it.

c James replies '25' when Kirstie gives him a number. Write down the equation this gives and solve it.

4 Billy pays £5 for four cups of tea, which includes a tip of £1. Using c for the price of a cup of tea, write down the equation this gives and solve it.

5 A rectangle has a perimeter of 24. The length is twice as long as the width, w.

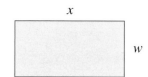

a Write an expression for the length x in terms of w.

b Write an equation from the information given about the perimeter of this rectangle.

c Solve this equation to find the length and width of the rectangle.

6 Solve each of the following problems by creating an equation and then solving it.

a The sum of two consecutive even numbers is 54, find the numbers.

b If the sum of two consecutive odd numbers is 208, what are the numbers?

c John weighs 3 kg more than his brother. Their total weight is 185 kg. How much does John weigh?

d Joy's Auntie Mary is four times as old as Joy. If the sum of their ages is 70, find their ages.

e The sum of six consecutive even numbers is 174. What is the smallest of the numbers?

f The sum of seven consecutive odd numbers is 133. What is the largest of the numbers?

Extension Work

1 The sum of two numbers is 56, and their difference is 14. What are the two numbers?

2 The sum of two numbers is 43, and their product is 450. What are the two numbers?

3 The difference of two numbers is 12, and their product is 448. What is their sum?

4 The sum of two numbers is 11, and twice the first plus half the second is 10. Find the product of the two numbers.

Lines and equations

Look at the diagram on the right.

The coordinates on the dashed line are:

(0, 4) (1, 4) (2, 4) (3, 4) (4, 4) (5, 4) (6, 4)

Notice that the second number, the y-coordinate, is 4 every time.

Therefore, the dashed line is said to have the equation:

$y = 4$

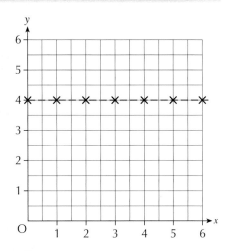

Now look at the next diagram on the right.

The coordinates shown in this dashed line are:

(2, 0) (2, 1) (2, 2) (2, 3) (2, 4) (2, 5) (2, 6)

Notice that the first number, the x-coordinate, is 2 every time.

Therefore, the dashed line is said to have the equation:

$x = 2$

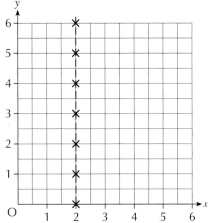

Exercise 13D

1 Look at each diagram. Write out the coordinates shown on each dashed line; and state its equation.

a

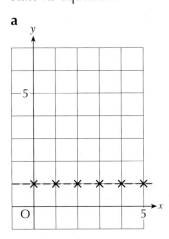

b

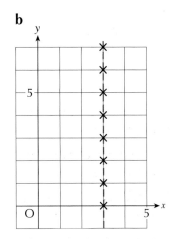

c

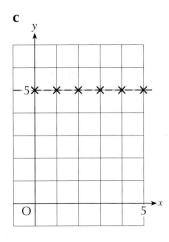

2 Draw simple diagrams to show the straight lines with the following equations:

a	$y = 2$	**b**	$x = 3$
c	$y = 3$	**d**	$x = 1$
e	$x = 6$	**f**	$y + 5$

3 Draw a grid with each axis from 0 to 5.

   i Draw each pair of lines given below on the grid.

   ii Write down the coordinates of the point where each pair of lines cross.

     a $x = 1$ and $y = 3$ **b** $x = 2$ and $y = 4$ **c** $x = 5$ and $y = 1$

     d What do you notice about the crossing coordinates for each pair of lines?

     e Work out the coordinates of the point where the following lines cross:
       $x = 17$ and $y = 28$

4 Look at each diagram.

   a
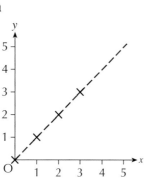

   b
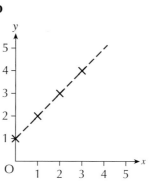

   c
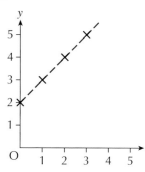

   d
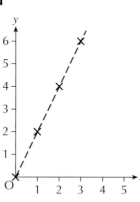

   e
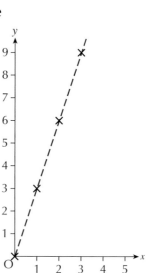

   f
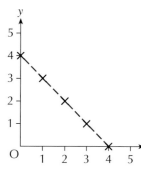

   i Write down the coordinates of each of the points marked on the dashed lines.

   ii Do you notice anything special about the numbers?

   iii In each case, try to write the rule that converts y to x.

Extension Work

   a Write down at least four coordinates (x, y) that fit the rule $y = 2x + 1$.

   b Draw a suitable grid, plot these points and draw the straight line that joins the points.

   c Repeat the above to draw lines with the following equations.

     i $y = 2x + 3$ **ii** $y = 2x + 5$ **iii** $y = 2x + 4$

Real-life graphs

Graphs are used to show a relationship that exists between two variables.

Example 13.6 ▷ Draw a sketch graph to illustrate that a hot cup of tea will take about 20 minutes to get cold.

The graph is shown below. The two axes needed are Temperature and Time, with time on the horizontal axis and graduated in minutes.

The temperature starts at Hot at 0 minutes, and is at Cold after 20 minutes.

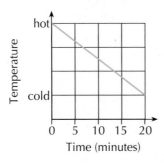

Note The graph has a **negative gradient**. That is, it slopes downwards from left to right.

Exercise 13E

1. Sketch a graph to illustrate each of the following comments. Clearly label each axis.

   a The more sunshine we have, the hotter it becomes.

   b The longer the distance, the longer it takes to travel.

   c In 2 hours all the water in a saucer had evaporated.

   d My petrol tank is full at the start of a journey full, with 40 litres of petrol in it. When my journey has finished, 300 miles later, my tank is nearly empty. It has just 5 litres of petrol left in it.

2. The graph shows a car park's charges.

   a How much are the charges for each of these stays?
      i 30 minutes
      ii Less than 1 hour
      iii 2 hours
      iv 2 hours 59 minutes
      v 3 hours 30 minutes
      vi 6 hours

   b For how long can a person park for each of these amounts?
      i £1   **ii** £2   **iii** £5

   c This type graph is called a step graph. Explain why it is given this name.

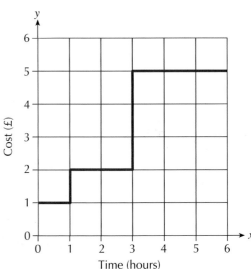

3 A country's parcel post costs are given in the table shown.

Weight	Cost
0 grams to 500 grams	£1.00
Above 500 grams and up to 1 kg	£2.50
Above 1 kg and up to 2 kg	£3.00
Above 2 kg and up to 3 kg	£4.50
Above 3 kg and up to 5 kg	£7.00

Draw a step graph to show charges against weight.

4 Look at each of the following graphs and write a short story to go with it.

a

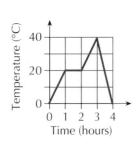

b

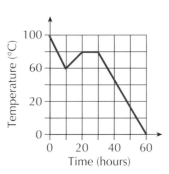

c

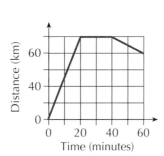

d

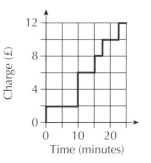

Extension Work

A taxi's meter reads £2 at the start of every journey. Once 2 miles has been travelled, an extra £3 is added to the fare. The reading then increases in steps of £3 for each whole mile covered up to five miles. For journeys over 5 miles, an extra £1 is added per mile over the five

a How much is charged for the following journeys?
  i Half a mile   **ii** 1 mile   **iii** 3 miles
  iv 5 miles   **v** 6 miles   **vi** 10 miles

b Draw a step graph to show the charges for journeys up to 10 miles.

Change of subject

Look at the following formula:

$$P = 4a + 2b$$

The formula states the value of the variable P, in terms of a and b.

P is called the **subject** of the formula. Often, a formula has to be rearranged to make another variable into the subject.

This is done in a similar way to solving an equation, by writing out its mapping, then finding the inverse mapping and working that through.

Example 13.7

Change the formula $E = 5t + 3$ to make t the subject.

Start the mapping from t:

$$t \longrightarrow \boxed{\times 5} \longrightarrow \boxed{+3} \longrightarrow E$$

Now write the inverse mapping:

$$t \longleftarrow \boxed{\div 5} \longleftarrow \boxed{-3} \longleftarrow E$$

This gives:

$$t = \frac{E - 3}{5}$$

Note how the division by 5 is shown.

Example 13.8

Rewrite the formula $N = 2m - p$ to express m in terms of N and p.

Start the mapping from m:

$$m \longrightarrow \boxed{\times 2} \longrightarrow \boxed{-p} \longrightarrow N$$

Now write the inverse mapping:

$$m \longleftarrow \boxed{\div 2} \longleftarrow \boxed{+p} \longleftarrow N$$

This gives:

$$m = \frac{N + p}{2}$$

Exercise 13F

1. Rewrite each of the following formulae as indicated.

   a. $A = w + k$. Express w in terms of A and k.

   b. $A = hb$. Express h in terms of A and b.

   c. $C = 3r + D$. Express r in terms of C and D.

   d. $P = 2a + 2b$. Express a in terms of P and b.

2 Rewrite each of the following formulae as indicated.

    a $C = pD$. Make D the subject of the formula.

    b $V = 2o + 5t$. Make t the subject of the formula.

    c $S = 3h + 2k$. Make h the subject of the formula.

    d $V = 4p - k$. Make k the subject of the formula.

    e $S = 5t + 4$. Make t the subject of the formula.

3 $E = 5n + 8$

    a   Find E when $n = 15$.

    b   Make n the subject of the formula.

    c   Find n when $E = 23$.

4 $S = a + 3t$

    a   Find S when $a = 7$ and $t = 4$.

    b   Make t the subject of the formula.

    c   Find t when $S = 24$ and $a = 6$.

5 $y = 5t - p$

    a   Find y when $t = 2$ and $p = 3$.

    b   Make t the subject of the formula.

    c   Find t when $y = 12$ and $p = 8$.

6 $V = 12rh$

    a   Find V when $r = 5$ and $h = 2$.

    b   Make r the subject of the formula.

    c   Find r when $V = 36$ and $h = 2$.

7 Use the formula $T = 7m + 4k$ to find the value of k when $m = 3$ and $T = 33$.

Extension Work

How quickly can you add together all the whole-numbers (integers) from 1 to 1000?

There are three ways which you may like to try.

a   Adding up all of them (this is likely to take a long time!)

b   Using pairs of numbers to help you to add them up.
    For example $1 + 1000 = 1001$, $2 + 999 = 1001$, etc.

c   Using a spreadsheet.

What you need to know for level 4

- How to use inverse mappings
- How to expand simple brackets
- How to plot and interpret coordinates

What you need to know for level 5

- How to construct and use simple formulae
- How to solve simple linear equations
- How to simplify expressions that involve simple, like terms

National Curriculum SATs questions

LEVEL 5

1 *2000 Paper 2*

Joanne is cooking dinner. Her rule for working out how much rice to cook is:

Number of spoonfuls of rice = Double the number of people and then add one.

For example: For three people she cooks seven spoonfuls of rice

Write Joanne's rule as a formula. Use S for the number of spoonfuls of rice and P for the number of people.

2 *1999 Paper 1*

The diagram shows a rectangle $(n + 3)$ cm long and $(n + 2)$ cm wide. It has been split into four smaller rectangles.

Copy the diagram and write a number or an expression for the area of each small rectangle.

One has been done for you:

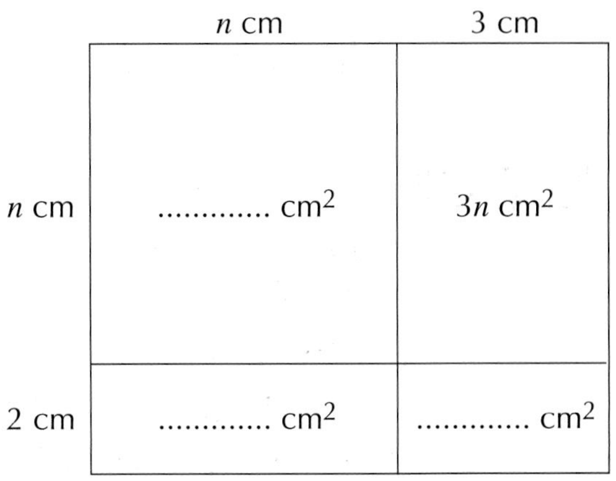

n cm
3 cm
n cm
.... cm²
3n cm²
2 cm
.... cm²
.... cm²

This chapter is going to show you

- how to investigate problems involving numbers and measures
- how to identify important information in a question
- how to interpret information from tables
- how to use examples to prove a statement is true or false
- how to use proportion or ratio

What you should already know

- When to use symbols or words to describe a problem
- When to use tables, diagrams and graphs
- How to break down a calculation into simpler steps
- How to find examples to match a statement

Number and measures

A leaflet has 12 pages. The pages have stories, adverts or both on them. Half of the pages have both. The number of pages which have adverts only is twice the number of pages which have stories only. How many pages have stories only?

Example 14.1   Use the digits 1, 2 and 3 and the multiplication sign × once only to make the largest possible answer.

Write down different examples:

$1 \times 32 = 32$	$1 \times 23 = 23$
$2 \times 31 = 62$	$2 \times 13 = 13$
$3 \times 21 = 63$	$3 \times 12 = 12$

The largest possible answer is $3 \times 21 = 63$.

1 Two consecutive numbers add up to 13. What are the numbers?

2 **a** Copy and complete the table.

Powers of 3	Working out	Answer	Units digit
3^1	3	3	3
3^2	3×3	9	9
3^3	$3 \times 3 \times 3$	27	7
3^4	$3 \times 3 \times 3 \times 3$	81	1
3^5	$3 \times 3 \times 3 \times 3 \times 3$	243	
3^6			
3^7			
3^8			

b What is the units digit of 3^{12}?

3 A dog and a cat run around a circular track of length 24 m. They both set off in the same direction from the starting line at the same time. The dog runs at 6 m per second and the cat runs at 4 m per second. How long is it before the dog and the cat are together again?

4 **a** Use your calculator to find two consecutive odd numbers which multiplied together give an answer of 143.

b Use the digits 1, 3 and 4 and the multiplication sign × once only to make the largest possible answer.

5 Here is a magic square. Each row, column and diagonal adds up to 15.

8	1	6
3	5	7
4	9	2

Complete these magic squares so that each row, column and diagonal adds up to 15.

4		8
	7	

2		4
7		

6		7
6		

6 Amy is 6 years older than Bill. The sum of their ages is 16 years. How old will Amy be in 4 years' time?

7 A map has a scale of 1 cm to 3 km. The road between two towns is 5 cm on the map. Calculate the actual distance between the two towns.

8 Which is the greater mass, 3 kg or 7 pounds (lb)? Use the fact that 1 kg ≈ 2.2 lb.

9 Which is the greater length, 10 miles or 15 kilometres? Use the fact that 5 miles ≈ 8 kilometres.

10 Which is the greater area, 1 square mile or 1 square kilometre? Explain your answer.

Make up a recipe in imperial units. For example: 6 ounces of flour, 2 pints of water, etc. Use metric conversions and rewrite the recipe in metric units. If you need to find out the conversions, use a textbook or the Internet.

Using words and diagrams to solve problems

There are three chickens A, B and C. A and B have a total mass of 5 kg. A and C have a total mass of 6 kg. B and C have a total mass of 7 kg. What is the mass of each chicken?

Example 14.2

A gardener charges £3 per hour. Write down a formula, in words, for the total charge when the gardener is hired for several hours. Work out the cost of hiring the gardener for 6 hours.

The formula is:

The charge is equal to the number of hours worked multiplied by three pounds

If the gardener is hired for 6 hours, the charge = 6 × £3

= £18

So, the charge is £18.

Example 14.3

I think of a number, add 3 and then double it. The answer is 16. What is the number?

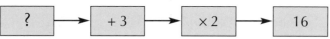

Working this flowchart backwards gives:

The answer is 5.

Exercise 14B

1 A man and his suitcase weigh 84 kg. The suitcase weighs 12 kg. What is the weight of the man?

2 Two numbers add up to 43. One of the numbers is 19. What is the other number?

3 a A tool hire company charges £8 per day to hire a tool. Write down a formula, in words, for the total charge when a tool is hired for a number of days.

b Work out the cost for 10 days.

c A different company uses a table to work out their charges.

1 day	2 to 3 days	4 to 5 days	More than 5 days
£12	£10 per day	£8 per day	£7.50 per day

Use the table to work out the total cost of hiring a tool from this company for

i 3 days   **ii** 5 days   **iii** 8 days

4 I think of a number, double it and add 1. The answer is 19.

Work the flow diagram backwards to find the number.

5 I think of a number, multiply it by 3 and subtract 5. The answer is 25.

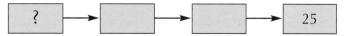

    a Copy and complete the flow diagram.

    b Work backwards to find the number.

6 I think of a number, divide it by 2 and add 5. The answer is 11.

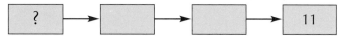

    a Copy and complete the flow diagram.

    b Work backwards to find the number.

7 Each year a man invests £50 more than the year before. In the first year he invested £100.

    a How much does he invest in the tenth year?

    b How much has he invested altogether after ten years?

8

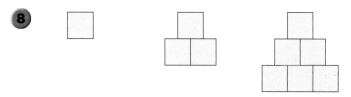

    a Draw the next pattern in the sequence.

    b How many squares will the fifth pattern have?

    c Write down a rule to work out the number of squares in the next pattern.

9 A grid has 100 squares. If the squares are labelled 0, 1, 2, 3, 4, 5, ... , what is the label on the 100th square? Explain how you know.

10 There are 32 teams in a knockout tournament. In the first round there will be 16 matches. How many matches will there be altogether?

Extension Work

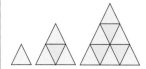

Equilateral triangles are pieced together to make a pattern of triangles as shown. The first diagram has only one small triangle. How many small triangles are in the next two patterns? Extend the patterns to see if you can work out a formula for the number of small triangles in the tenth pattern. What is the special name given to this pattern?

Logical solutions and best value

Look at the recipe. This is for four people. How much of each ingredient is needed to make a chocolate cake for eight people?

Chocolate cake
500g flour
100g sugar
35g cocoa powder
60g butter

Example 14.4 ▷ Give an example to show that any even number multiplied by any other even number always gives an even number.

Two examples are:

$2 \times 4 = 8$ $10 \times 6 = 60$

Both 8 and 60 are even numbers.

Example 14.5 ▷ Take any three consecutive numbers. Add the first number to the third number and divide the answer by 2. What do you notice?

Take, for example, 1, 2, 3 and 7, 8, 9. These give:

$1 + 3 = 4$ $7 + 9 = 16$
$4 \div 2 = 2$ $16 \div 2 = 8$

Whichever three consecutive numbers you choose, you should always get the middle number.

Exercise 14C

1 Copy and complete each of the following number problems, filling in the missing digits:

a
```
    3 □
  + □ 7
  ─────
    4 9
```

b
```
    4 □
  + □ 3
  ─────
    7 6
```

c
```
    1 3 □
  +   □ 7
  ───────
    □ 4 9
```

d
```
    8 □
  - □ 2
  ─────
    4 5
```

e
```
    2 3 8
  - □ □ □
  ───────
    1 1 7
```

f
```
    □ 3 5
  ×     4
  ───────
    5 □ □
```

2 Write down an example to show that when you add two odd numbers, the answer is always an even number.

3 Write down an example to show that when you add two even numbers, the answer is always an even number.

4 Write down an example to show that when you add an odd number to an even number, the answer is always an odd number.

5 Write down an example to show that when you multiply together two odd numbers, the answer is always an odd number.

6 Write down an example to show that when you multiply an odd number by an even number, the answer is always an even number.

7 Which bottle is the best value for money?

FIZZ 1 litre £1.25

FIZZ 2 litres £2.40

FIZZ 4 litres £4.95

8 Which is the better value for money?

a 6 litres for £12 or 3 litres for £9.

b 4 kg for £10 or 8 kg for £18.

c 200 g for £4 or 300 g for £5.

d Six chocolate bars for £1.50 or four chocolate bars for 90p.

9 A recipe uses 250 g of meat and makes a meal for five people. How many grammes of meat would be needed to make a meal for 15 people?

Extension Work

Invent your own recipes for two people. Rewrite them for four people and then for five people. Remember that you cannot have half an egg!

Proportion

Look at the picture.
Can you work out how many pints are in 3 litres?

A litre of water is a pint and three-quarters

Example 14.6

A café sells 200 cups of tea, 150 cups of coffee and 250 other drinks in a day.

What proportion of the drinks sold are

a cups of tea? **b** cups of coffee?

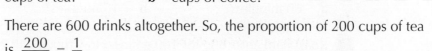

a There are 600 drinks altogether. So, the proportion of 200 cups of tea is $\frac{200}{600} = \frac{1}{3}$.

b There are 150 cups of coffee out of 600 drinks altogether. So, the proportion of cups of coffee is $\frac{150}{200} = \frac{1}{4}$.

1 An orange drink is made using one part juice to four parts water. What proportion of the drink is juice? Give your answer as a fraction, decimal or percentage.

2 A woman spends £75 on food and £25 on clothing. What proportion of her spending is on food?

3 A supermarket uses $\frac{3}{4}$ of its space for food and the rest for non-food items. What fraction does it use for non-food items?

4 A green paint is made by mixing three parts of blue paint with seven parts of yellow paint. How many litres of blue and yellow paint are needed to make:

    a   20 litres of green paint?   **b**   5 litres of green paint?

5 5 miles is approximately 8 km.

    a   How many miles are equal to 24 km?

    b   How many kilometres are equal to 25 miles?

6 30 cm is approximately 1 foot.

    a   How many feet are 120 cm?

    b   How many feet are 15 cm?

    c   How many feet are 45 cm?

7 Four cakes cost £10. What will twelve cakes cost?

8 Six towels cost £18. What will three towels cost?

9 Ten candles cost £12. What will 15 candles cost?

10 A lorry travels at 60 miles per hour on the motorway.

    a   How far will it travel in 3 hours?

    b   How far will it travel in 15 minutes?

    c   How far will it travel in 3 hours and 15 minutes?

11 In 15 minutes a car travelled 12 km. If it continued at the same speed, how far did it travel in:

    a   30 minutes?   **b**   45 minutes?   **c**   1 hour?

12 In 30 minutes, 40 litres of water runs through a pipe. How much water will run through the pipe in:

    a   60 minutes?   **b**   15 minutes?   **c**   45 minutes?

13 Roast ham costs 80p for 100 grams. How much will 250 grams cost?

Extension Work

Design a spreadsheet that a shopkeeper could use to double her prices.

Ratio

John and Mary are sharing out the sweets. John wants twice as many sweets as Mary, and there are 21 sweets altogether. Can you work out how many sweets each gets?

Example 14.7 Michael has 32 CDs. Alice has three times as many as Michael. How many CDs do they have altogether?

Alice has three times as many CDs as Michael, so Alice has 3 × 32 = 96 CDs.

This means that altogether they have 32 + 96 = 128 CDs.

Example 14.8 James and Briony are two goalkeepers. James has let in twice as many goals as Briony. Altogether they have let in 27 goals. How many goals has James let in?

You need to find two numbers that add up to 27. One number is double the other.

By trying different pairs of numbers, you will find that the answers are 18 and 9.

So, James has let in 18 goals.

Example 14.9 Alex has 21 pencils. The ratio of coloured pencils to black pencils is 2 : 1. How many coloured pencils does Alex have?

The ratio of 2 : 1 means that there are twice as many coloured pencils as there are black pencils.

By trying different pairs of numbers, you will find that the answers are 14 and 7.

So, Alex has 14 coloured pencils.

Example 14.10 Simplify each of these ratios.

    a 18 : 12   **b** 20 : 100   **c** 35 minutes : 15 minutes   **d** 2 cm : 25 mm

    a 18 and 12 will both divide by 6. So, 18 : 12 = (18 ÷ 6) : (12 ÷ 6)
$$= 3 : 2$$

    b 20 and 100 can be done in two stages. First divide by 10 and then by 2.
$$20 : 100 = 2 : 10 \; (\div 10)$$
$$= 1 : 5 \;\; (\div 2)$$

    c When units are in a ratio, they can be ignored when both units are the same. So, in this case:
$$35 \text{ minutes} : 15 \text{ minutes} = 35 : 15$$
$$= (35 \div 5) : (15 \div 5)$$
$$= 7 : 3$$

    d When the units are different, one unit must be changed to make it the same as the other unit. So, in this case:
$$2 \text{ cm} : 25 \text{ mm} = 20 \text{ mm} : 25 \text{ mm}$$
$$= 20 : 25$$
$$= 4 : 5$$

1 Simplify each of these ratios:

a	6 : 4	**b**	10 : 25	**c**	21 : 7	**d**	6 : 9
e	5 : 20	**f**	8 : 2	**g**	12 : 3	**h**	20 : 15
i	4 : 12	**j**	32 : 8	**k**	15 : 3	**l**	100 : 25
m	400 : 1000	**n**	500 : 1000	**o**	100 : 70	**p**	100 : 750
q	120 : 30	**r**	24 : 6	**s**	20 : 300	**t**	50 : 250

2 Simplify each of these ratios.

a	6 hours : 4 hours	**b**	10 minutes : 25 minutes	**c**	21 days : 7 days
d	6 kg : 9 kg	**e**	5 cm : 20 cm	**f**	8 litres : 2 litres

3 Simplify each of these ratios.

a	1 hour : 30 minutes	**b**	15 minutes : 1 hour	**c**	1 week : 7 days
d	1 kg : 200 g	**e**	20 mm : 1 cm	**f**	1 litre : 2000 ml

4 Harriet and Richard go shopping. Altogether they buy 66 items. Harriet buys twice as many items as Richard. How many items does Harriet buy?

5 At a concert there are half as many males as females. There are 240 people altogether. How many females are at the concert?

6 180 people see a film at the cinema. The number of children to the number of adults are in the ratio 2 : 1. How many children see the film?

7 In a fishing contest the number of trout caught to the number of carp caught is in the ratio 1 : 2. The total number of trout and carp is 24. How many carp were caught?

8 A bakery makes 1200 loaves. The ratio of white to brown is 3 : 1. How many brown loaves did the bakery make?

9 A do-it-yourself shop sells paints. The ratio of gloss paint to emulsion paint sold on one day is 1 : 3. If they sell 80 litres of paint, how much gloss paint do they sell?

Extension Work

Draw a cube of side 1 cm. Now draw a cube of side 2 cm.

 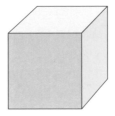

Investigate what happens to the total length of all the edges of a cube as you double its dimensions.

The surface area of the small cube is 6 cm² as there are six faces. Work out the surface area of the bigger cube. Then investigate what happens when you double its dimensions.

Extend the problem to a cube of side 3 cm. Then consider cuboids.

National Curriculum SATs questions

LEVEL 4

1   *1997 Paper 2*

The grid shows the first eight lines of a spiral pattern. The spiral pattern starts at the point marked ■.

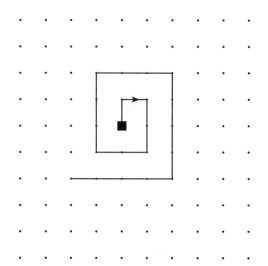

a   Continue the spiral by drawing the next four lines on the grid below.

b   The table shows the length of each line.

Line number	Length
1	1
2	1
3	2
4	2
5	3
6	3
7	4
8	4
9	5

The rule for finding the length of odd numbered lines is:

Line number ⟶ +1 ⟶ ÷2 ⟶ Length

What is the length of the line number 23?

c   Fill in the box to show the rule for finding the length of even numbered lines.

Line number ⟶ ☐ ⟶ Length

d   What is the length of line number 18?

2   Sue and Ben each have 12 biscuits.

    a   Sue eats a quarter of her biscuits. How many biscuits does Sue eat?

    b   Ben eat 6 of his 12 biscuits. What fraction of his biscuits does Ben eat?

    c   How many biscuits are left altogether?

LEVEL 5

3   *1998 Paper 2*

You can make different colours of paint by mixing red, blue and yellow in different proportions.

For example, you can make green by mixing 1 part blue to 1 part yellow.

    a   To make purple, you mix 3 parts red to 7 parts blue. How much of each colour do you need to make 20 litres of purple paint? Give your answer in litres.

    b   To make orange, you mix 13 parts yellow to 7 parts red. How much of each colour do you need to make 10 litres of orange paint? Give your answer in litres.

4   *1999 Paper 2*

    a   Nigel pours one carton of apple juice and three cartons of orange juice into a big jug.

       What is the ratio of apple juice to orange juice in Nigel's jug?

    b   Lesley pours one carton of apple juice and $1\frac{1}{2}$ cartons of orange juice into another big jug.

       What is the ratio of apple juice to orange juice in Lesley's jug?

    c   Tandi pours one carton of apple juice and one carton of orange juice into another big jug.

       She wants only half as much apple juice as orange juice in her jug.
       What should Tandi pour into her jug now?

5   You can work out the cost of an advert in a newspaper by using this formula:

$C = 15n + 75$
    C is the cost in £
    n is the number of words in the advert

    a   An advert has 18 words. Work out the cost of the advert. Show your working.

    b   The cost of an advert is £615. How many words are in the advert? Show your working.

This chapter is going to show you

- how to draw plans, elevations and scale drawings
- how to solve problems using coordinates
- how to construct a triangle given three sides
- how to find a locus
- how to use bearings
- how to solve problems with cuboids

What you should already know

- How to draw nets of 3-D shapes
- How to plot coordinates
- How to construct triangles from given data
- How to measure and draw angles
- How to calculate the surface area of cuboids

Plans and elevations

A **plan** is the view of a 3-D shape when it is looked at from above. An **elevation** is the view of a 3-D shape when it is looked at from the front or from the side.

Example 15.1 ▷

The 3-D shape shown is drawn on isometric dotted paper. Notice that the paper must be used the correct way round, so always check that the dots form vertical columns.

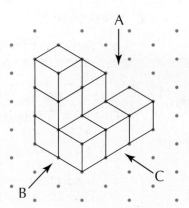

The plan, front elevation and side elevation can be drawn on squared paper:

Plan from **A**

Front elevation from **B**

Side elevation from **C**

1 Draw each of the following cuboids accurately on an isometric grid:

a
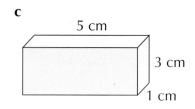
2 cm
2 cm
2 cm

b
4 cm
3 cm
2 cm

c
5 cm
3 cm
1 cm

2 Copy each of the following 3-D shapes onto an isometric grid:

a

b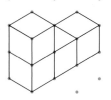

c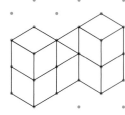

d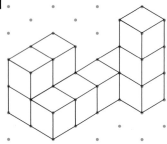

e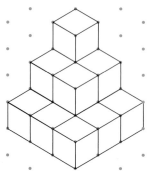

For each one, draw on centimetre-squared paper:

i the plan   **ii** the front elevation   **iii** the side elevation

3 The plan, front elevation and side elevation of a 3-D solid made up of cubes, are shown below:

Plan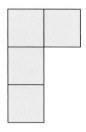

Front elevation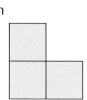

Side elevation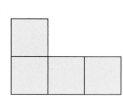

Draw the solid on an isometric grid.

4 The diagrams below are the views of various 3-D shapes from directly above:

a   **b**   **c**   **d**   **e**   **f**

For each one, write down the name of a 3-D shape that could have this plan.

5 Make a 3-D solid from multi-link cubes. On centimetre-squared paper draw its plan, front elevation and side elevation and show these to a partner. Ask your partner to construct the solid using multi-link cubes. Compare the two solids made.

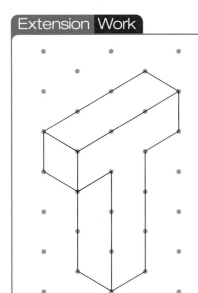

The letter 'T' is drawn on an isometric grid, as shown on the left:

a Draw other capital letters that can be drawn on an isometric grid.

b Explain why only certain capital letters can be drawn easily on the grid.

c Design a poster, using any of these letters, to make a logo for a person who has these letters as their initials.

Scale drawings

A **scale drawing** is a smaller drawing of an actual object. A scale must always be clearly given by the side of the scale drawing.

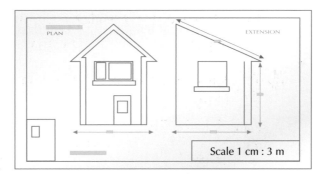

Example 15.2

This is a scale drawing of Rebecca's room.

- On the scale drawing, the length of the room is 5 cm, so the actual length of the room is 5 m.

- On the scale drawing, the width of the room is 3.5 cm, so the actual width of the room is 3.5 m.

- On the scale drawing, the width of the window is 2 cm, so the actual width of the window is 2 m.

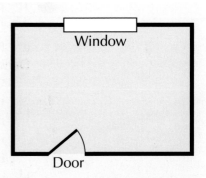

Scale: 1 cm to 1 m

1 The lines shown are drawn using a scale of 1 cm to 10 m. Write down the length each line represents:

a ────────
b ──────────────────
c ───────────────
d ──────────────────────
e ─────────────────

2 The diagram shows a scale drawing for a school hall:

a Find the actual length of the hall.
b Find the actual width of the hall.
c Find the actual distance between the opposite corners of the hall.

Scale: 1 cm to 5 m

3 The diagram shown is Ryan's scale drawing for his Mathematics classroom. Nathan notices that Ryan has not put a scale on the drawing, but he knows that the length of the classroom is 8 m:

a What scale has Ryan used?
b What is the actual width of the classroom?
c What is the actual area of the classroom?

4 Copy and complete the table below for a scale drawing in which the scale is 4 cm to 1 m.

	Actual length	Length on scale drawing
a	4 m	
b	1.5 m	
c	50 cm	
d		12 cm
e		10 cm
f		4.8 cm

5 The plan shown is for a bungalow:

a Find the actual dimensions of each of the following rooms:
  i the kitchen
  ii the bathroom
  iii bedroom 1
  iv bedroom 2
b Calculate the actual area of the living room.

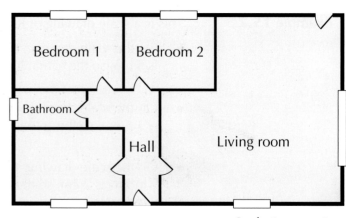

Scale 1 cm to 2 m

6 The diagram shows the plan of a football pitch. It is not drawn to scale. Use the measurements on the diagram to make a scale drawing of the pitch (choose your own scale).

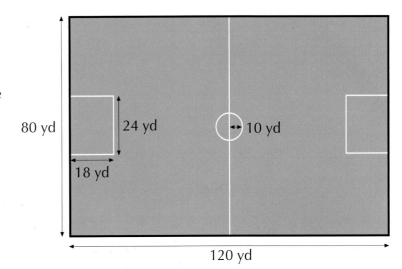

80 yd

24 yd

10 yd

18 yd

120 yd

Extension Work

1   On centimetre-squared paper, design a layout for a bedroom. Make cutouts for any furniture you wish to have in the room (use a scale of 2 cm to 1 m).

2   You will need a metre rule or a tape measure for this activity. Draw a plan of your classroom, including the desks and any other furniture in the room. Choose your own scale.

Coordinates in all four quadrants

We use **coordinates** to locate a point on a grid.

The grid consists of two axes, called the *x*-axis and the *y*-axis. They are perpendicular to each other.

The two axes meet at a point called the **origin**, which is labelled O.

The point A on the grid is 4 units across and 3 units up.

We say that the coordinates of A are (4, 3), which is usually written as A(4, 3).

The first number, 4, is the *x*-coordinate of A and the second number, 3, is the *y*-coordinate of A. The *x*-coordinate is *always* written first.

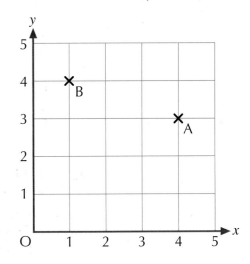

When plotting a point on a grid, a ✗ is usually used.

The coordinates of the origin are (0, 0) and the coordinates of the point B are (1, 4).

The grid system can be extended to negative numbers and points can be plotted in all **four quadrants**.

Example 15.3 ▷ The coordinates of the points on the grid are:

A(4, 2), B(–2, 3), C(–3, –1), D(1, –4)

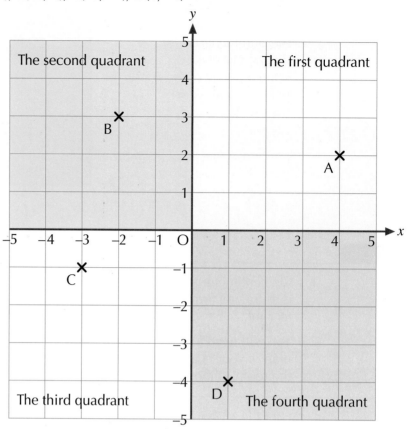

1 Write down the coordinates of the points P, Q, R, S and T.

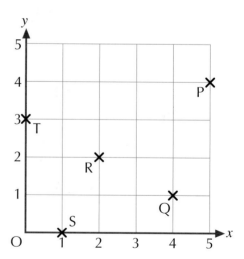

2 **a** Make a copy of the grid in Question 1. Then plot the points A(1, 1), B(1, 5) and C(4, 5).

b The three points are the vertices of a rectangle. Plot the point D to complete the rectangle.

c Write down the coordinates of D.

3 Write down the coordinates of the points A, B, C, D, E, F, G and H.

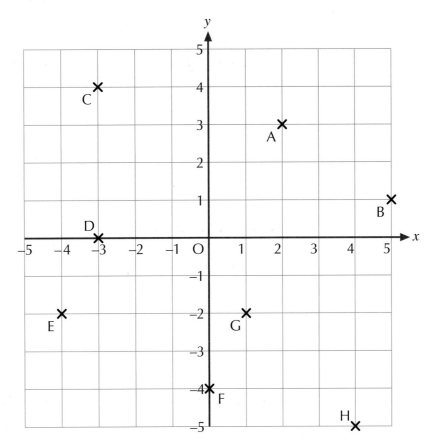

4 a Make a copy of the grid in Question 3. Then plot the points A(–4, 3), B(–2, –2), C(0, 1), D(2, –2) and E(4, 3).

Constructing triangles

In Year 7, you learned how to construct triangles, using a ruler and a protractor, from given data. You were able to construct the following:

- a triangle given two sides and the included angle (SAS):

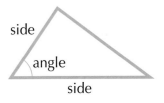

- a triangle given two angles and the included side (ASA):

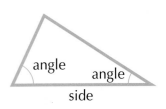

The example below shows you how to construct a triangle given three sides (SSS). You need a ruler and compasses for this construction.

Example 15.4

To construct the triangle PQR.

Draw a line QR 6 cm long. Set compasses to a radius of 4 cm and, with centre at Q, draw a large arc above QR.

Set compasses to a radius of 5 cm and, with the centre at R, draw a large arc to intersect the first arc. The intersection of the two arcs is P.

Join QP and RP to complete the triangle. Leave your construction lines on the diagram.

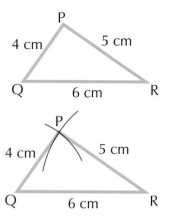

1 Construct each of the following triangles (remember to label all the sides and angles):

a

b

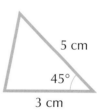

c

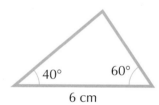

d

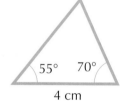

2 Construct each of the following triangles (remember to label all the lines):

a

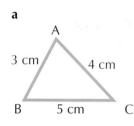

b

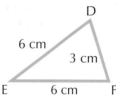

c

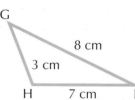

d

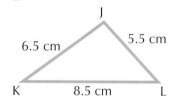

3 Construct the ΔXYZ with XY = 7 cm, XZ = 4 cm and YZ = 6 cm.

4 Construct the ΔPQR with PQ = 5 cm, QR = 12 cm and PR = 13 cm. What type of triangle have you drawn?

5 Construct equilateral triangles with sides of length:

   a 3 cm   **b** 5 cm   **c** 4.5 cm

6 Paul thinks that he can construct a triangle with sides of length 3 cm, 4 cm and 8 cm, but finds that he cannot draw it:

   a Try to construct Paul's triangle.
   b Explain why it is not possible to draw Paul's triangle.

1 Construct the quadrilaterals shown using only a ruler and compasses:

a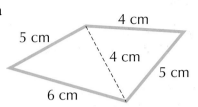

b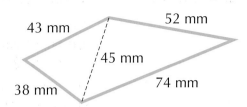

2 a Draw the net below accurately on card. Cut out the net to make a square-based pyramid. Make the square 4 cm by 4 cm, and each equilateral triangle 4 cm by 4 cm by 4 cm.

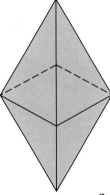

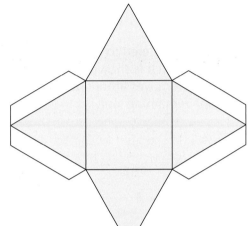

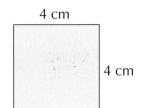

b Construct another two square-based pyramids and paste their bases together to make an octahedron, like the one in the diagram.

3 If you have access to ICT facilities, find out how to construct triangles using programs such as LOGO.

Loci

The trail from the jet aircraft has traced out a path. The path of the trail is known as a **locus**. A locus (the plural is **loci**) is a set of points that satisfies a given set of conditions or a rule. It is useful to think of a locus as a path traced out by a single moving point.

Example 15.5 ▷ Mr Yeates is walking along a straight path that is equidistant from two trees (equidistant means 'the same distance'). The sketch below shows the locus of his walk along the path. In some cases, the locus can be drawn accurately if measurements are given.

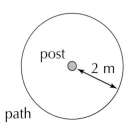

tree   tree

Example 15.6 ▷ Mr McGinty's goat is tethered to a post by a rope 2 m long. A sketch is shown of the locus of the goat as it moves around the post with the rope remaining taut.

post
2 m

path

The locus can be described as a circle with a radius of 2 m.

Exercise 15E

1 Draw a sketch and describe the locus for each of the following situations:

   a   The path of a cricket ball being hit for a six by a batsman.
   b   The path of the Earth as it orbits the sun.
   c   The path of a bullet from a rifle.
   d   The path of the tip of Big Ben's minute hand as it moves from 3 o'clock to half past three.
   e   The path of a parachutist after jumping from a plane.
   f   The path of the pendulum of a grandfather clock.

2 Barn A and barn B are 500 m apart. A farmer drives his tractor between the barns so that he is equidistant from each one. On a sketch of the diagram, draw the locus of the farmer.

barn A   barn B

◄───────────────── 500 m ─────────────────►

3 The diagram on the right shows two fences that border a park. Kathryn enters the park at an entrance at X. She then walks through the park so that she is equidistant from each fence.

On a sketch of the diagram, draw the locus of Kathryn.

X

4 A toy car starts at point A at the edge of a room, and moves so that it is always a fixed distance from point Y.

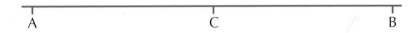
A ———————— Y

a On a sketch of the diagram, draw the locus of the car.
b Describe the locus of the car.

5 The line AB is 20 cm long and C is its mid-point.

A   C   B

a Describe the locus of A if the line is rotated about C.
b Describe the locus of A if the line is rotated about B.

Extension Work

1 The diagram on the right shows the dimensions of a building. A path is to be laid around the building so that the edge of the path is always 1 m away from the building. Make a scale drawing to show the edge of the path around the building (use a scale of 1 cm to 1 m).

8 m

2 m

6 m

5 m

2 The diagram shows the position of two car-park meters in a large car park in a city centre. When Mrs Kitson buys her parking ticket, she always walks to the nearest meter. On a sketch of the car park, divide the car park into two regions to show the nearest meter available depending on where she parks.

3 Use reference material or the Internet to find out about contours, isotherms and isobars. How are these related to a locus?

4 If you have access to ICT facilities, find out how to generate shapes and paths, using programs such as LOGO. For example, find out how to draw regular polygons, star shapes and spiral shapes.

Bearings

There are four main directions on a compass – north (N), south (S), east (E) and west (W). These directions are examples of **compass bearings**.

Bearings are mainly used for navigation purposes at sea, in the air and in sports such as orienteering. A bearing is measured in degrees (°) and the angle is always measured **clockwise** from the **north lines**. The symbol for due north is: ↑

You have probably seen this symbol on maps in Geography.

A bearing is always given using three digits and so is sometimes referred to as a three-figure bearing. For example, the bearing for the direction east is 090°.

Example 15.7 On the diagram, the three-figure bearing of B from A is 035° and the three-figure bearing of A from B is 215°.

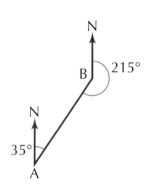

Example 15.8 The diagram shows the positions of Manchester and Leeds on a map.

The bearing of Leeds from Manchester is 050° and the bearing of Manchester from Leeds is 230°. Notice that the two bearings have a difference of 180°; such bearings are often referred to as 'back bearings'.

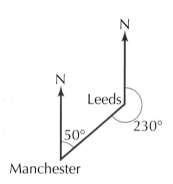

Exercise 15F

1 Write down each of the following compass bearings as three-figure bearings:

    a south   **b** west   **c** north-east   **d** south-west

2 Write down the three-figure bearing of B from A for each of the following:

  a   **b**   **c**   **d**

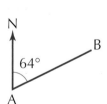 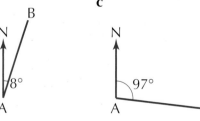 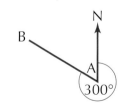

3 Find the three-figure bearing of X from Y for each of the following:

a 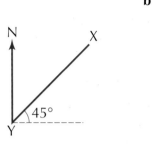 **b**  **c** 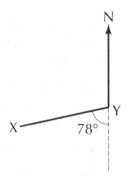 **d**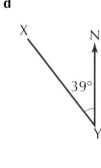

4 Draw a rough sketch to show each of the bearings below (mark the angle on each sketch):

    a   From a ship A, the bearing of a light-house B is 030°.

    b   From a town C, the bearing of town D is 138°.

    c   From a gate E, the bearing of a trigonometric point F is 220°.

    d   From a control tower G, the bearing of an aircraft H is 333°.

5 The two diagrams show the positions of towns and cities in England.

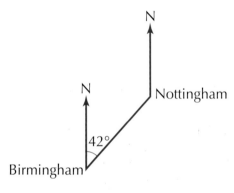

    Find the bearing of each of the following:

    a **i**   Nottingham from Birmingham

         ii Birmingham from Nottingham

    b **i**   Scarborough from Blackpool

         ii Blackpool from Scarborough.

Extension Work

A liner travels from a port X on a bearing of 140° for 120 nautical miles to a port Y. It then travels from port Y on a bearing of 250° for a further 160 nautical miles to a port Z.

    a   Make a scale drawing to show the journey of the liner (use a scale of 1 cm to 20 nautical miles).

    b   Use your scale drawing to find:

         i   the direct distance the liner travels from port Z to return to port X.

         ii the bearing of port X from port Z.

A cube investigation

For this investigation you will need a collection of cubes and centimetre isometric dotted paper.

Two cubes can only be arranged in one way to make a solid shape, as shown.

Copy the diagram onto centimetre isometric dotted paper. The surface area of the solid is 10 cm².

Three cubes can be arranged in two different ways, as shown.

Copy the diagrams onto centimetre isometric dotted paper. The surface area of both solids is 14 cm².

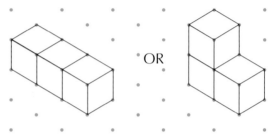

OR

Here is an arrangement of four cubes:

The surface area of the solid is 18 cm².

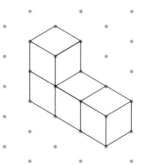

How many different arrangements can you make using four cubes?

Draw all the different arrangements on centimetre isometric dotted paper.

What is the greatest surface area for the different solids you have made?

What is the least surface area for the different solids you have made?

Draw a table to show your results and write down anything you notice.

What do you think are the greatest and least surface areas of a solid made from five cubes?

What you need to know for level 4

o How to use coordinates in the first quadrant

What you need to know for level 5

o How to use coordinates in all four quadrants
o How to make a scale drawing
o How to use three-figure bearings
o How to draw simple plans and elevations
o How to find the surface area of a cuboid

National Curriculum SATs questions

LEVEL 4

1 *2000 Paper 1*

Look at the shaded shape.

a Two statements below are correct.
Write down the correct statements.

The shape is a quadrilateral.

The shape is a trapezium.

The shape is a pentagon.

The shape is a kite.

The shape is a parallelogram.

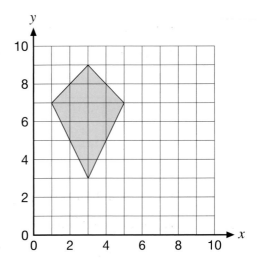

b What are the coordinates of point B?

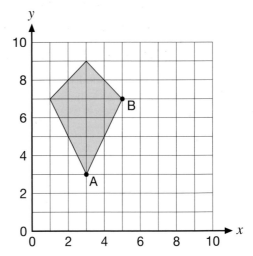

LEVEL 5

2 *2001 Paper 2*

A plan of a ferry crossing is shown.

a Draw an accurate scale drawing of the ferry crossing (use a scale of 1 cm to 20 m).

b What is the length of the ferry crossing on your diagram?

c The scale is 1 cm to 20 m. Work out the length of the real ferry crossing. Show your working, and write the units with your answer.

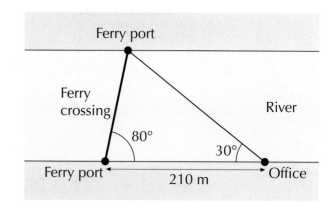

3 *1997 Paper 2*

Alex is making a box to display a shell.

The base of the box is shaded.

He draws the net of the box like this:

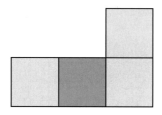

Alex wants to put a lid on the box.

He must add one more square to his net.

a Make three copies of the diagram on the right. On each one show a different place to add the new square for the lid. Remember that the base of the box is shaded.

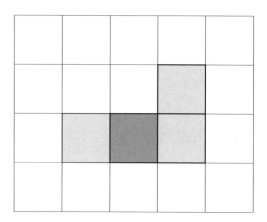

b Alex makes a different box with a lid hinged at the top.

The base of his box is shaded.

Draw a full size net for his box.

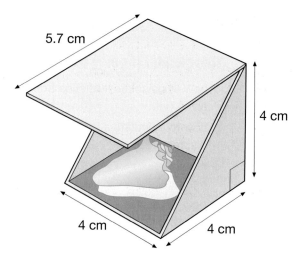

5.7 cm

4 cm

4 cm

4 cm

CHAPTER 16 — Handling Data 3

This chapter is going to show you

○ how to calculate statistics from given data

○ how to calculate a median for discrete data

○ how to construct frequency diagrams for discrete data

○ how to compare two distributions by using an average and the range

○ how to compare theoretical probabilities with experimental probabilities

What you should already know

○ How to construct frequency tables for discrete data

○ How to find the mode and range for discrete data

○ How to calculate the mean for discrete data

○ How to construct simple bar charts

Frequency tables

There are three equal periods in an ice hockey game. Use the picture to work out the time on the clock at the end of each period.

Example 16.1 The waiting times, in minutes, of people at a bus stop are shown below.

2, 5, 1, 8, 7, 6, 5, 1, 8, 7
2, 1, 0, 0, 2, 8, 7, 5, 6, 5

Construct a frequency table to represent the data.

The table can be set out either across the page in two rows or down the page in two columns. There were two people who waited 0 minutes, three people who waited for 1 minute, three people who waited for 2 minutes and so on.

Putting all this information in the table gives:

Waiting time (minutes)	0	1	2	3	4	5	6	7	8
Number of people	2	3	3	0	0	4	2	3	3

Example 16.2 ▷ Use the data given in Example 16.1 to complete the table for grouped data.

Waiting time (minutes)	0–2	3–5	6–8
Number of people			

The data is now going to be grouped so that the people who waited 0, 1 or 2 minutes are counted together. Those who waited 3, 4 or 5 minutes are counted together. So are those who waited 6, 7 or 8 minutes.

The completed table gives:

Waiting time (minutes)	0–2	3–5	6–8
Number of people	8	4	8

Exercise 16A

1 The length of time 25 customers spend in a shop is recorded:

Time (minutes)	Number of customers
0–10	12
11–20	7
21–30	6

Two more customers enter the shop. The first customer is in the shop for 5 minutes and the second customer is in the shop for 21 minutes.

Copy and update the table to include these two customers.

2 The heights (in metres) of 20 people are given below.

1.6, 1.5, 1.7, 1.6, 1.4, 1.7, 1.5, 1.5, 1.8, 1.8
1.5, 1.6, 1.8, 1.6, 1.4, 1.7, 1.7, 1.6, 1.6, 1.7

a Copy and complete the frequency table.

Height (metres)	Tally	Number of people
1.4–1.5		
1.6–1.7		
1.8–1.9		

b Which class interval contains the most people?

3 The masses (in kilograms) of fish caught in one day by a fisherman are shown below

1, 5, 3, 4, 6, 1, 2
4, 5, 1, 5, 4, 3, 3

a Copy and complete the frequency table.

Mass (kilograms)	Tally	Number of fish
0–2		
3–5		
6–8		

b Which class interval contains the least fish?

4 The temperature (in °C) of 16 towns in Britain is recorded on one day:

12, 10, 9, 13, 12, 14, 17, 16

18, 10, 12, 11, 15, 15, 12, 13

a Copy and complete the frequency table:

Temperature (°C)	Tally	Frequency
8–10		
11–13		
14–16		
17–19		

b Which class interval contained the most common temperature?

Extension Work

Record the number of pages in a large number of school textbooks. Decide on suitable class intervals for the data to be collected together into a frequency table. Complete the table. Comment on your results.

The median

When dealing with data you often need to find an average. The mode, the median and the mean are all types of average.

This section explains how to find the median.

The median is the middle value for a set of values when they are put in numerical order.

Example 16.3 Here are the scores of nine players in a quiz. Find the median.

12, 11, 9, 14, 13, 9, 6, 17, 14

First, put the scores in order: 6, 9, 9, 11, 12, 13, 14, 14, 17.
The median is the number in the middle of the set. So, the median is 12.

Example 16.4 Below are the marks of twelve pupils in an English test.

17, 16, 19, 16, 15, 14, 18, 20, 14, 18, 17, 16

First, put the marks in order:

14, 14, 15, 16, 16, 16, 17, 17, 18, 18, 19, 20

There are two numbers in the middle of the set: 16 and 17. The median is the number in the middle of these two numbers. So, the median is 16.5.

Exercise 16B

1 Find the median of each of the following sets of data.

a 4, 6, 3, 4, 5, 1, 8, 6, 6

b 21, 27, 22, 24, 27, 21, 23, 26, 25, 25, 24

c 7, 11, 6, 15, 12, 11, 10

d 102, 108, 106, 110, 98, 94, 109, 111, 105

2 Find the median of each of the following sets of data.

   a   14, 17, 15, 16, 18, 12

   b   3, 6, 4, 6, 3, 7, 0, 2, 6, 8

   c   84, 62, 73, 77

   d   112, 110, 109, 115, 113, 108

3 Find the median of each of the following sets of data.

   a   18 kg, 20 kg, 23 kg, 18 kg, 24 kg

   b   £1.50, £2.20, £1.78, £2.36, £1. 47

   c   104 cm, 105 cm, 103 cm, 102 cm, 108 cm, 100 cm

   d   35 litres, 14 litres, 20 litres, 24 litres

4 **a**   Write down a list of five numbers which has a median of 10.

   b   Write down a list of seven numbers which has a median of 8.

   c   Write down a list of six numbers which has a median of 14.

   d   Write down a list of ten numbers which has a median of 12.

5 A group of swimmers are sponsored for swimming lengths of the pool.

Here is the number of lengths that each swimmer completes:

   17   12   23   8   7   17   18   22   30

Find the median number of lengths for this data.

6 Six students compare how much money they have brought to school.

Here are the amounts: £0, £2, £1.80, £0, £3, £3.60

Work out the median amount for these six students.

Extension **Work**

Ask people in your class to tell you the name of their favourite pop band or solo artist. Write down both their answer and the number of people in the band (one if it is a solo artist). When you have collected all your data, find the median number of people in the bands.

Drawing frequency diagrams

Look at the picture. How could you record the different ways in which students travel to school?

When data has been collected from a survey, it can then be displayed using different diagrams to make it easier to understand.

Bar charts can be used to show different categories, such as walking to school, using the school bus or going to school by taxi. This bar chart would have gaps between the bars.

Bar charts can also be used for grouped data. For example, when recording word lengths for 100 words, the number of letters per word can be grouped into categories, such as 1–3, 4–6, 7–9 and 10–12.

Bar-line graphs are used to show single values. A typical case would be, when rolling a dice 50 times, record the number of times that each score (1, 2, 3, 4, 5 or 6) is obtained.

Example 16.5

Construct a bar chart for the following data about the ways in which students travel to school.

How students travel to school	Number of students
Walk	4
Bus	5
Car	10
Cycle	6

It is important that the bar chart has a title and is labelled, as shown below.

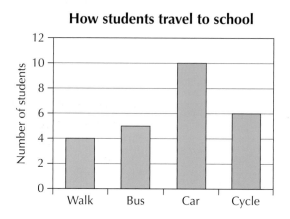

Example 16.6

A dice is rolled 50 times. Construct a bar-line graph to show the results

The length of each bar represents each frequency. Do not join the tops of the bars.

Score on dice	Frequency
1	8
2	7
3	7
4	9
5	11
6	8

Score on a dice rolled 50 times

1 **a** Use the data in the frequency table to draw a bar chart to show the birthday season of a class of Year 8 students.

Birthday	Frequency
Spring	3
Summer	6
Autumn	8
Winter	7

b Use the data in the frequency table to draw a bar chart to show the favourite field event of competitors.

Field event	Frequency
Javelin	12
Discus	6
Shot	8
Hammer	9

c Use the data in the frequency table to draw a bar-line graph to show the scores out of 5 in a test.

Score in test	Frequency
0	9
1	12
2	6
3	3
4	7
5	1

d Use the data in the frequency table to draw a bar chart to show the number of words in 50 sentences.

Number of words	Frequency
0–10	8
11–20	12
21–30	25
31–40	5

2 The dual bar graph shows the mean monthly temperature for two cities.

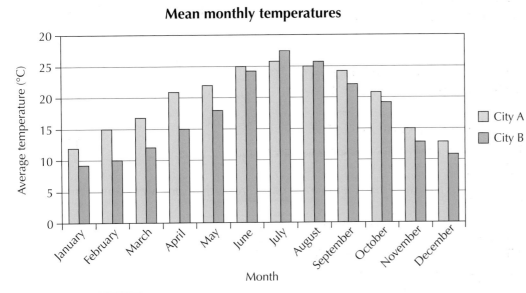

Mean monthly temperatures

a Which city has the highest mean monthly temperature?

b Which city has the lowest mean monthly temperature?

c How many months of the year is the temperature higher in City A than City B?

d What is the difference in mean temperature between the two cities in February?

Extension Work

Use a travel brochure to compare the temperatures of two European resorts. Make a poster to advertise one resort as being better than the other.

Comparing data

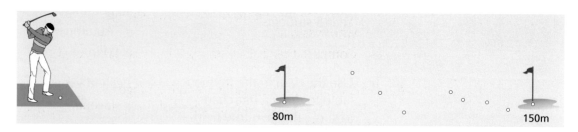

80m   150m

Look at the picture. What is the range of the golfer's shots?

Example 16.7 ▷ The table shows the mean and range of basketball scores for two teams.

Compare the mean and range. What do they tell you?

	Team A	Team B
Mean	75	84
Range	20	10

The mean tells you that the average score for Team B is higher than that for Team A. So Team B has higher scores generally.

The range is the difference in their lowest and highest scores. As this is higher for Team A, there is a greater variation in Team A's scores. That is, Team A is less consistent than Team B.

Exercise 16D

1 The temperature of melting ice is 0 °C and the temperature of boiling water is 100 °C. What is the range of the two temperatures?

2 The times of four students in a 100-metre race are recorded as:
14.2 s, 13.8 s, 15.1 s, 17.3 s

Write down the range of the times.

3 A factory worker records the start and finish times of a series of jobs:

Job number	1	2	3	4	5
Start time	9.00 AM	9.20 AM	9.50 AM	10.10 AM	10.20 AM
Finish time	9.15 AM	9.45 AM	10.06 AM	10.18 AM	10.37 AM

Work out the range of the times taken for each job.

4 The minimum and maximum temperatures are recorded for four counties in England in April:

County	Northumberland	Leicestershire	Oxfordshire	Surrey
Minimum	2 °C	4 °C	4 °C	4.5 °C
Maximum	12 °C	15 °C	16.5 °C	17.5 °C

a Find the range of the temperatures for each county.
b Comment on any differences you notice.

5 The table shows the mean and range of a set of test scores for Jon and Matt.

	Jon	Matt
Mean	64	71
Range	35	23

    a   Compare the means of the scores, stating who was better.

    b   Compare the ranges, stating who was more consistent.

6 The table shows the medians and the ranges of the scores of Kyle and Lisa after playing on a computer game.

	Kyle	Lisa
Median	875	1500
Range	200	650

    a   Compare the medians of their scores, stating who you think is the better player.

    b   Compare the ranges, stating who is more consistent.

7 The table shows the mode and range of shoe sizes for men and women in a high-street shop.

	Men	Women
Mode	9	6
Range	8	7

    Compare the modes and the ranges. What do they tell you.

8 Belinda bought three bottles of wine. The total price was £18 and the range was £2.50. The cheapest bottle cost £4.50.

    a   What was the cost of the most expensive bottle?

    b   What was the cost of the other bottle?

Extension Work

Use an atlas or another data source (the Internet or a software program) to compare the population and area of China with the population and area of the United States of America.

Which average to use?

Look at the queue of people. Why is it impossible to find the most common height?

This table will help you decide which type of average to use for a set of data.

	Advantages	Disadvantages	Example
Mean	Uses all the values. The most widely used average.	May not be representative when the data contains extreme values.	1, 1, 1, 2, 4, 15 Mean $= \dfrac{1 + 1 + 1 + 2 + 4 + 15}{6} = 4$ which is a higher value than most of the data.
Median	Uses only the middle value, so it is a better average to use when the data contains extreme values.	Not all values are used, so could be misleading.	1, 1, 3, 5, 10, 15, 20 Median = 4th value = 5 Note that the median is close to the values 1, 1 and 3 but further from the values 10, 15 and 20.
Mode	Most frequently occurring value. Can be used for non-numerical data	When the mode is an extreme value, it is misleading to use it as an average. May not exist.	Weekly wages of a boss and his four staff: £150, £150, £150, £150, £1000. Mode is £150 but mean is £320.
Range	Measures how spread out the values are.	Uses the two most extreme values.	1, 2, 5, 7, 9, 40. Range 40 – 1 = 39 Without the last value (40), the range would be only 8.

1. Look at each set of data and the average which has been calculated. Say whether you think it is a suitable average to use.

   a   3, 3, 5, 7, 8, 10   Mean = 6
   b   0, 1, 2, 2, 2, 4, 6   Mode = 2
   c   1, 4, 7, 8, 10, 11, 12   Median = 8
   d   2, 3, 6, 7, 10, 10, 10   Mode =10
   e   2, 2, 2, 2, 14, 16, 28   Median = 2
   f   0, 1, 4, 6, 9, 100   Mean = 20

2. The time (in seconds) to complete a short task is recorded for each of 15 students.

   10, 10, 10, 10, 11, 11, 12, 12, 12, 13, 14, 15, 15, 16, 17

   The values are then grouped into a frequency table.

   a   Write down the mode.
   b   The median is 13. Explain why the median is more useful than the mode in this case.

Time (Seconds)	Frequency
10	4
11	2
12	3
13	1
14	1
15	2
16	1
17	1

3 Look at each set of data and decide whether the range is a suitable representation of each set or not. Explain your answer.

   a   1, 2, 4, 7, 9, 100
   b   9, 10, 10, 10, 11
   c   1, 100, 101, 102, 104
   d   1, 3, 5, 6, 7, 10
   e   1, 1, 1, 7, 10, 10, 10
   f   2, 5, 8, 10, 14

Extension **Work**

Collect the attendances at English Premiership football matches over one weekend. Calculate the range of this set of data.

Repeat this exercise for the Scottish Premier division.

Compare the differences in the distributions of the data. Explain why the range is probably more suitable for the English division than the Scottish division.

Repeat the calculations but ignore the largest attendance in each division. What effect does this have on your answers?

Experimental and theoretical probability

Look at the picture. Would you say that there is an even chance of the jigsaw pieces coming out of the box face up, or do more pieces come out face down every time?

Example 16.8   Design and carry out an experiment to test whether drawing pins usually land with the pin pointing up or the pin pointing down.

Count out 50 drawing pins, then drop them onto a table.

Record the number with the pin pointing up and the number with the pin pointing down.

Suppose that 30 point up and 20 point down.

We could then say that the experimental probability of a pin pointing up is:

$$\frac{30}{20} = \frac{3}{5} = 0.6.$$

Exercise 16F   ① Darren says that when people are asked to think of a number between 1 and 10 inclusive, they will pick 3 or 7 more often than any other number.

   a   Carry out an experiment to test Darren's prediction by asking first 10 people and then 20 people.

   b   Compare your results with the theoretical probability, which is $\frac{2}{10} = 0.2$.

2 a Carry out an experiment with an ordinary dice by recording the number of times that it lands on 6 after 30 throws.

b Compare your results with the theoretical probability of a fair dice, which is $\frac{1}{6} = 0.167$.

3 Five cards, numbered 1, 2, 3, 4 and 5, are placed face down in order, in a row. Cards are picked at random.

A gambler predicts that when people pick a card they will rarely pick the end ones.

a Carry out an experiment 20 times to test his prediction.

b Compare your results with the theoretical probability, which is

P (end card) $= \frac{2}{5} = 0.4$.

4 The theoretical probability that a coin lands on its Head is $\frac{1}{2}$.

Toss a coin 40 times and record the results. State whether you think that your coin is fair.

Extension Work

Use computer software to simulate an experiment: for example, tossing a coin or rolling a dice. Work out the experimental probabilities after 10, 20, 30 results have been obtained. Then compare them with the theoretical probability. Write down any pattern that you notice. Repeat the experiment to see whether any pattern is repeated.

What you need to know for level 4

- How to collect discrete data and record it using a frequency table
- Understand the meaning of the mode and the median, and how to use them
- How to construct and interpret simple line graphs

What you need to know for level 5

- Understand and use the mean of discrete data
- How to find and justify probabilities based on equally likely outcomes and experimental evidence, as appropriate
- Understand that different outcomes may result from repeating an experiment

National Curriculum SATs questions

LEVEL 4

1 *2000 Paper 1*

    a The diagram shows spinner A and spinner B.

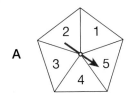 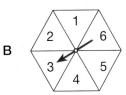

Which spinner gives you the best chance to get 1?

      Spinner A   Spinner B   Doesn't matter

Explain why you chose your answer.

    b Here are two different spinners. The spinners are the same shape but different sizes.

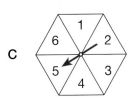 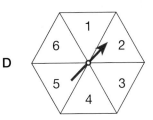

Which spinner gives you the best chance to get 3?

      Spinner A   Spinner B   Doesn't matter

Explain why you chose your answer.

    c Each section of spinner E is the same size. Copy spinner E and fill in numbers so that both of these statements are true.

        It is equally likely that you will spin 3 or 2.

        It is more likely that you will spin 4 than 2.

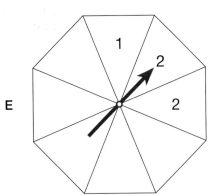

LEVEL 5

2 *2000 Paper 2*

    a   Paula played four games in a competition.

        In three games, Paula scored 8 points each time. In the other game she scored no points.

        What was Paula's mean score over the four games?

    b   Jessie only played two games.

        Her mean score was 3 points. Her range was 4 points.

        What points did Jessie score in her two games?

    c   Ali played three games.

        His mean score was also 3 points. His range was also 4 points.

        What points might Ali have scored in his three games? Show your working.

3 *1998 Paper 2*

Some students threw three fair dice.

They recorded how many times the numbers on the dice were the same.

Name	Number of throws	Results		
		All different	Two the same	All the same
Morgan	40	26	12	2
Sue	140	81	56	3
Zenta	20	10	10	0
Ali	100	54	42	4

    a   Write the name of the student whose data are most likely to give the best estimate of the probability of getting each result. Explain your answer.

    b   This table show the students' results collected together:

Number of throws	Results		
	All different	Two the same	All the same
300	171	120	9

Use these data to estimate the probability of throwing numbers that are all different.